MW01493341

Angels Among Us
The Fabulous J. Oliver Black

By

Evelyn "Betty" Howard

Published in the United States of America
by Ariadne Publishers, Brookfield, WI, U.S.A.
ISBN: 9781729165768

Contents

Chapter 1 – I Meet My Guru

I WAS MAGNETIZED by his luminous face, his infectious laughter, his divine love and friendship. Shortly after I met him, as he came down the aisle, I saw him suddenly turn into dazzling light; at the same time, a strange force almost caused me to fall at his feet. Before that could actually happen, I saw him return to his normal appearance. But when I awakened from my shock — this being the first of many spiritual experiences which I was to  undergo — I realized I was being given a message that this was a pure soul in the eyes of God and that I lacked humility and respect.

Later, he made known to me that he knew me better than I knew myself — my weaknesses and my strengths, the skeletons in my closet. Everything about me was known to him; there were no secrets. I felt very disconcerted. There was nowhere to hide, and I soon found out there was no fooling him; he knew my every thought.

One day, as we were all seated around him and he was at the end of the table, I began to mull over these thoughts in my head — who was he? I felt he seemed to be omniscient, omnipotent, omnipresent. I saw him answering people's questions with great wisdom. Miraculous things would happen around him. I realized I could feel his presence in Chicago, where I lived, even though he was in Detroit. So I was thinking to myself, he must be *God,* for he seems to have the power of God. Just at this point, my reverie was abruptly broken by his voice. I looked up. His piercing eyes were focused on me as he stopped right in the middle of his conversation with the people next to him and said, "Well, I'll tell you one thing. *God* isn't a man." He made it a natural part of his conversation, as he taught everyone around him.

Just to be around him was to experience spiritual inspiration and illumination. He radiated peace, divine love, and spiritual strength.

One day I brought my mother to meet him. On the way there, she kept referring to Bible passages and asked me, "What's the matter with Christ?" She thought there was something wrong with me for idolizing Yogacharya the way I did. When he stepped up to the podium, he began to give equivalent passages from yoga philosophy to all the biblical quotes she had just brought up to me. At the end of the service as we gathered around him, my mother wanted to stay back, for she sensed that he knew her thoughts. But he didn't let her escape. He said, "Come on, Mother, you sit right here," as he held a chair for her right beside his. It wasn't long before she too was magnetized by his love, just like the rest of us.

One day I brought a friend who was a devout Catholic. Although I didn't know it, she had decided in her own mind that if this was a man of God, she would feel great bliss just being in his presence. After the service ended and we all gathered around for fellowship with him, there she was. She hadn't felt the bliss; she just didn't know what to think. Suddenly, as we were standing there, she did feel it; she later described it as "a great all-encompassing feeling of bliss dawned on me." He reached out his hand to her arm and asked, "How's that?" She has never forgotten this great spiritual moment and to this day believes and knows that he was, indeed, a man of God.

Another time I brought a man to see him who was depressed and dispirited. After the service, I saw him shaking hands with Yogacharya. He later told me, "As I shook his hand, I felt an electric spiritual current go up my spine." Afterwards, as we gathered around to talk, Yogacharya told of a Jackie Gleason comedy show where a "yogi" character got drunk and fell onto a bed of nails and that alcohol fumes spurted out of the holes. Then he laughed heartily. I wondered, what was this story all about? On the way home the young man told me he felt the story was meant for him, as he had gotten drunk that week. Yogacharya was telling him that alcohol and yoga studies just don't mix. Still later, the young man also gave up his habit of chain smoking. Due to the spiritual influence exerted by Yogacharya Oliver, he became a changed person, no longer depressed and unhappy. He overcame his depression and once again became full of life and vigor. He began to practice yoga meditation and sometimes got up at 3:00 a.m. to commune with God, as he heard Yogacharya did.

Still another time I brought a child to him for healing; the child was only six years old and was diagnosed with advanced cancer. Yogacharya assured me he had no powers, and he held his hands together as though forming a pipe and said, "It's like this," I took it to mean he felt he was a channel, not the Power. He said healing was God's business, not his. Moreover he said, "You cannot know what's behind every angelic looking face." He instructed me not to bring people to him for healing, for he could not do it. In my mind I kept feeling he could, I knew he could. And the little boy did get markedly better for about six months before he died.

When I first came to see Yogacharya, I was looking for someone spiritually advanced enough to heal me. I felt sure I had cancer of the breast. I was terribly depressed and sure that I wouldn't be alive after another six months. He had this habit of picking people up somehow by standing in back of them, putting his hands under their arms and around their neck. He would give a

Betty and Yogacharya, 1967.

4

little shake and something in their spine would make a snapping sound. It was a sight to see. It was a cure-all for everything I was to find out years later. And it was a cure-all for me as well, for from that day forth, I developed a strong conviction that I was getting better. I completely lost my fears of dying, and, after several years, the lumps too went away.

Often a group of us from Chicago would travel to his Sunday service in Detroit. Enroute you'd find us talking about all sorts of things. Somehow when we'd reach Detroit, we'd find him talking about the same things we had talked about in the car, whether it was about Dale Carnegie, or George Washington Carver, or whatever. It just seemed that there wasn't a thought that missed him.

Once there was a young man whom I took to meet him who was all tied up in knots. He had a nervous stomach and lots of other problems. Yogacharya talked at length to the group that morning. Later, the young man told me, "It was like he was talking directly to me." He was so thrilled with the many answers he got to his problems. Yogacharya's method of teaching often came through parables or anecdotes.

Another woman with problems I took to meet him turned to me and said, "He's describing just like it is at my office." She, too, got her answer. Paramahansa Yogananda expressed it thus: "The weary, weak, and heavy laden, Oliver, they are yours."

People came from far and near all with grave problems. He would seemingly know about each and all. Somehow all of their problems got resolved. He

5

understood us all and knew exactly the direction we were going. He never tried to change our individual bent. He just gave love and friendship. The way became clear to everyone who came. He was a delight to be around, and more than that, the greatest blessings came in the love he expressed to all. None of us will ever forget this unique and fabulous spirit.

For years before my first meeting with Yogacharya, I had sought to find a spiritual teacher whose feet were not of clay. I finally found my teacher in Yogacharya, a.k.a., J. Oliver Black, retired car parts manufacturer. He had been a very successful businessman in his early years. By the time I met him he was a full-time minister of the Self Realization Fellowship yoga movement.

I first met Yogacharya in 1959 after I had been studying the Self -Realization weekly lessons for about a year. I found this yoga philosophy seemed to literally personify my way of thinking. Yoga means union with God. I had a desire to know God better. The path was a set of disciplines, the practice of love, self-mastery, and meditation was the avenue. I liked this philosophy, which seemed to me more of a science than a religion. If you agreed with what was said, you'd incorporate it in your way of living. If not, you'd throw it out. By this practice I found I was becoming more peaceful, happy and loving. I felt this was the right path for me.

When I met Yogacharya I intuitively knew he was a master. A master is one who has learned to master himself, not others. He had great wisdom, laughed a lot and was very blissful. I listened to everything he had to say as we gathered around him after the Sunday services in Detroit. I was fascinated. He kept us spellbound. That first year, even though I lived in Chicago at the time, I attended services every week. His countenance was always luminous. I couldn't take my eyes off him. His eyes seemed like flames reaching down to his soul. I was transfixed by his magnetism, his divine love, his humility and sweetness. I was sure God had finally led me to that all-encompassing, beautiful soul whom I had been seeking for so long.

Before coming to my first service, I had reached a place in the lessons where I felt I'd like to attend the Kriya service and commit myself to joining Self-Realization Fellowship. I liked the teaching that one needs to go within and become acquainted with the inner, God-self. This made good sense to me, for I had been inspired by Christ's words, "The things I do, if you believe, you also can do, and greater things shall you do." Christ had said, "The Kingdom of God is within you." "As a man thinketh in his heart, so is he." These statements were intriguing to me. I reasoned that if one could learn to love as Christ had loved, he would come to have the consciousness of Christ. Jesus said he had overcome the world and he admonished us to "Be ye therefore perfect." Since orthodox churches did not go far enough into these approaches to the inner life to suit me, I left them. I saw Jesus as a way shower and set out to follow his way, never for a minute thinking that it was impossible.

After I left the church, and for about eight years before I ever met the teacher God had sent me, Yogacharya, I had been getting up at 3:00 or 4:00 a.m.

doing what I called "meditation." Really, it was a reaching out and a listening process, not meditation, as my teacher taught me, later.

Yogacharya believed everyone knew right from wrong, so he allowed everyone to go their own way; he never tried to change their natural bent, but he guided them on their chosen route.

After I had been attending services for about a month, and during one of my meditations, I heard a voice within saying, as clearly as I hear a physical voice, "Yogacharya is your guru." Now I was not really seeking a guru, since I'm not Indian. In fact, I did not really know what a guru was in the correct sense of the word, but I have since learned that a guru is one who knows God and can show the devotee the way.

I had read *Autobiography of a Yogi* by Paramahansa Yogananda a few years earlier. I had felt a great loving presence in my room at that time, so I took it for granted that Paramahansa Yogananda was my guru. But now, after hearing the voice within, I gave a lot of thought to the term. I liked the idea of having a guru, or spiritual teacher: As time went on, I felt very blessed to have made the acquaintance of such a pure soul deemed by God.

Although the Sunday services took place at the Art Institute in Detroit and I lived in Chicago, I somehow found myself traveling to Detroit every week for a long time. I even used my rent money to make the trip one week! Yogacharya announced from the platform the start of the movement in Chicago long before I ever started a meditation group in my apartment in Chicago.

Once I did start the group, I found young people seemed to be coming from everywhere who wanted to attend a meditation group. I would take them all to meet Yogacharya. Our routine became that we would meet weekly to meditate at my apartment, and once a month we would all go to Detroit. Because his spiritual consciousness was so highly developed, we found that just being in his presence was enlightening. We found ourselves returning to Chicago renewed and refreshed, filled with inspiration to be a great light in the world.

After a few months, I began to go to a Thursday night service which Yogacharya conducted. So also, some of our more ardent Chicago members would go every Sunday. We would get together to discuss all the things we were experiencing and learning.

During these first few months, and after the experience of hearing the voice guiding me to Yogacharya as my guru, I went through many spiritual experiences. But first, I found myself depressed about my physical condition. I had developed lumps in both breasts and was sure I had cancer. One day, before I left for Detroit, I played a recording by Mario Lanza, "I'll Walk with God." In despair, I began to cry. Then I left for my regular trip to Detroit.

After the service ended, Yogacharya took us to get refreshments. I was so engrossed in my self-despair, I didn't even notice where we were going. When I began to look around me, I found we were in a place that looked to me like a night club. There were about ten of us seated around a table in a large room, with many other tables surrounding us. There was a platform at the end of the room with a band, and a vocalist. I felt a moment of panic. What are we doing in a night club? I wondered. Just at that moment, the vocalist began singing "I'll Walk with God." I was incredulous. I turned to Yogacharya who was sitting opposite to me. He was staring at me. He must have known I was about to burst into tears. I wanted to get up and run out, when suddenly I felt my tears and fears disappear like magic. I felt calmness descend, and I felt at peace with myself. What had happened? I felt in control of myself once more.

From the time of that magical moment, I started to get better. I now had a strong conviction that I was on the mend. The healing was not instantaneous. It took a few years, but gradually, imperceptibly, I became completely well.

About this same time, the Mother Center of Self-Realization Fellowship in Los Angeles, California, was holding a Kriya service, at which time devotees traveled to California to receive initiation and join the organization. I had been studying their lessons for a year, and I decided to go. But one had to fill out a questionnaire and return it, in order to be eligible. Since I had not practiced each of the preliminary disciplines, I could not answer the questions about what effects I was receiving from practicing these disciplines. So, just before visiting Yogacharya for the first time, I found myself in dismay, talking to the picture of Paramahansa Yogananda during my meditation, "Well, if I'm to go for Kriya, tell me." And then, out of frustration, I threw down the picture.

When I arrived in Detroit, Yogacharya met me practically at the entrance. Before I could say a word, he said, "You come here for Kriya." I replied that I hadn't filled out the SRF questionnaire. He said, "That's all right." I was puzzled. "I'm not sure I'm ready," I said. His only reply was, "You're ready." And he walked away. It wasn't until much later that I realized he had answered every question I had put to the picture of Yogananda. This was another example of how I became aware that he knew my every thought.

After giving the matter more thought and much prayer, I did attend his Kriya ceremony and thus became a member of Self-Realization Fellowship (without the questionnaire!). As a member in Detroit, I was now able to attend the Kriya service in California and visit the Mother Center in Los Angeles.

During my time in California, I was told by one of the monks of the SRF Order that Yogacharya couldn't possibly be my guru, for Paramahansa Yogananda was the only guru. It was my mind, he said, that produced the words I heard. I had to think that over for a while. Meanwhile, the monk gave a lecture on the guru-disciple relationship. I realized that I had had no thought or desire about having a guru, so how could my mind have produced the message that Yogacharya was my guru? Besides this, everything the monk said about the guru-disciple relationship in his lecture applied exactly to my relationship with Yogacharya. Yogacharya had revealed to me that he knew everything of my past. He knew every skeleton in my closet. And, in fact, my whole life was like an open book to him. He knew all my weaknesses and my strengths and understood me better than I understood myself. While all this was quite disconcerting to me, at the same time it was a great blessing to know that someone knew me and understood me very well. This someone, moreover, had such divine love and divine caring that he seemed to be totally free of all ego. I felt blessed to call him my guru. It was ironic, because the monk's lecture that day cemented my understanding of the guru-disciple relationship with Yogacharya forever. From that day forth, I had a great feeling of security. I felt a divine presence within my consciousness wherever I was, Detroit, California, even in Chicago. I felt this great presence within me, leading me and teaching me every step of the way, even more in Chicago than in Detroit. I found myself getting mixed up with my great love for the man and my ever greater love for the presence that I felt when I did not see him. I felt a very great drive to know God better. Somehow, everywhere I went I felt a presence was coming through people, books, and my everyday experiences. These experiences all showed me the next step up the spiritual ladder.

Each time I came to Detroit, Yogacharya would reveal to me my lack of humility and also my bad temper. He would always do or say something that brought on my anger. I had read recently of a woman who prayed to God for patience, and God sent her a trying maid. I was able to understand. I went home feeling defeated every time, but resolved that I would overcome my anger and next time he would not be able to make me get angry. But, of course, that went on for many weeks and months, before I felt I had conquered my anger.

During the first two years of knowing Yogacharya, I always felt inspired and elated. I had a very great motivation in a spiritual direction. And there was that great loving presence within my consciousness, showing me the way to handle every challenge.

People tend to look toward people who think as they do. From the time I met Yogacharya, I always seemed to be surrounded by the kind of people who were a challenge to me. It was as if they represented a part of my character that needed correcting or lacked love and patience. It would seem this great presence would never run out of ways to bring tests. If I found myself going off in a wrong direction, I would feel a great separation from this presence, and I truly loved my oneness with it. Much as one gets feelings of conscience, I would be miserable until I was back in tune with this wonderful, loving presence.

This kind of bonding went on for about two years. I continued to be secure in listening and became more laid back. I attempted to let go and practiced an *agapic* type of unconditional love.

But, after about two years, I found I wasn't feeling as much elation and inspiration. This feeling of a presence would be snatched away, just when I thought it was there for me. I then discovered I had to put forth more effort at doing right before I could feel the presence once more.

One Sunday, when I went back to Detroit for the service and for a visit with my guru, I found myself getting very frustrated, and I irritably said to Yogacharya, "Are you supposed to be a doormat for everyone, and let everyone step on you?" He casually answered in a quiet, subdued manner, "Great saints don't mind being stepped on."

He always seemed to have the right answer, the answer that was meant for me, that I needed to hear. So, I went on trying to practice humility, even though most of the time it probably was mistaken for weakness by others.

Those who came to him quiet and shy, unable to manifest their true potential, he would encourage, build up their ego, give them some inspiration, a lift. As time went on, they too would become new, happier, and more confident people.

Humility, I found out, is surrender to God, but out of strength, not weakness or inability. The person who surrenders because he can't do anything must have the ego built up first. One can't give up what he doesn't have already. Anyway, I consoled myself that my guru was always knocking my ego because I had an extra supply!

Yogacharya was the greatest kind of teacher that anyone could be blessed to have. He seemed to be a pure channel of God with no ego of his own. He knew each and every one of the people who came to him. He never sought them out, but devotees would come to him from far and near. As soon as he saw them, he already seemed to know them well. To each and all he would give divine love and friendship. Soon, they were able to work out their problems. He knew the weaknesses and strengths of each, and his divine consciousness was like a mirror which revealed everything to him. They soon learned, as

I already knew, that he understood them completely. They found a bond with him that only he and that devotee understood. Such was the depth of his knowing and his way of teaching.

Even after I had been around him for only a month, I had experienced of his consciousness what I could only describe as omniscient, omnipresent, and omnipotent. He just seemed to know everything. I felt his presence in Chicago. I witnessed many miracles each time I came to see him.

Chapter 2 – My Guru's Way of Teaching

HE TOLD ME ONE DAY that I should read *Milarepa* and also the five books entitled *Life and Teachings of the Masters of the Far East*.

Milerepa was about a man who lived in Tibet. He had a guru named Marpa. Because Milarepa had practiced black magic before Marpa came into his life and had done many evil things, Marpa was very hard on Milarepa. In fact, Marpa treated him very badly indeed. When I bought the book, I did something I had never done before, I opened it in the middle and read. It didn't take me long to get the message. I thought to myself, well, I haven't practiced black magic, and this is a different age, a different time and clime. I went on to console myself that Yogacharya couldn't treat me as Marpa treated Milarepa, but now, thirty-five years later, I can truly say that he did — mentally he has given me the "Marpa treatment"!

Before I ever left Canada, where I was born and lived until I was 23 years of age, I once had an experience where I saw in an inner vision a line and circles surrounding it and at the same time I was given the knowledge that the line was myself and the circles were thoughts. I could perceive that one could do as they desired in this world; as long as they persisted in their beliefs and held to the power of their convictions no matter what, they could come up over all obstacles. As a result of this experience, I knew intuitively that we live in a thought world.

My harsh treatment from Yogacharya was in my thinking, or my responding. He used to say that we have "sticky minds." We let things stick there instead of letting them go through. For me it was hard to let go, for I had much ego to overcome.

My parents were English and I had learned to like challenges. Yogacharya knew that. I went up the spiritual ladder better by adversity, and he always seemed to provide that adversity. I would say to him that the reward for passing a test would be a greater test, then he'd throw me a crumb — a small compliment! But for the most part, my life with Yogacharya was full of ups and downs, and I loved it, for I was growing like a weed under his tutelage. He was the greatest kind of teacher anyone could be blessed to have, and I worshipped the ground he walked on, so great was my love for him.

Each devotee had a unique relationship with him known only by the devotee and teacher Yogacharya. Our growth was an inner experience. Spirituality is a growth from within, not a growth from without. And we all grew strong and competed to see who would become a saint first! Being around Yogacharya brought the greatest years of my life, and when he left us at the age of 96, he turned me away from himself and turned me toward God directly for instruction.

I also read the books *Life and Teachings of the Masters of the Far East.* If Yogacharya had not been the one to have recommended them, I would not have been able to believe them. To make them a reality in my life, I would need much more spiritual growth first.

Our meditation group in Chicago grew ever more loving and molded with Yogacharya's patient teaching and training every month. When people came to him and asked whether they should go into an ashram or convent, he would never discourage those who were bent on doing that, but if they sought his advice, then, at that time, he would discourage them. He felt they should stay in "the cement mixer" as he called the world outside the ashram. Life is an obstacle course, but that is how we grow and with Yogacharya's help, we'll make it.

Yogacharya founded a retreat in northern Michigan a few years after I met him. Young people would flock to it and live nearby. Pretty soon they were calling it "Karma City." They thought it was going to be all peace and quiet, but his manner of teaching and managing the retreat was a new experience for them. He would put people into jobs where they would open like a budding flower. You could see the change in each one from month to month. He always knew just exactly what made each one grow and go forth. One young man was very much "turned within," having been on drugs before he came to the retreat. Yogacharya put him to work in the kitchen. Being in such close contact with the girls in the kitchen, he learned much, and he became more outgoing every day. Today he is a chef in another state. He went on to make a profession out of cooking after he left Yogacharya's retreat. The young people would join the staff of the ranch (Yogacharya's retreat) unable to do much of anything practical. After a few years of residing there, they had learned to do everything. Yogacharya was a great taskmaster. Everyone loved him and was eager to please him. Through love and discipline they became lights in the world. Later, when they left after a few years, they went forth into all walks of life, always a great light for God, wherever they went. The girls would learn to cook and housekeeping chores. Eventually, I was on the staff for a year and learned to cook there, and also to garden.

There was chanting and a quiet meditation every evening, and everyone had to attend. Meditation is attempting to quiet the mind and listen for God. After the meditation, we'd all gather around him, magnetized by his wisdom and divine love and friendship. There was a steady stream of people coming and going all the time: "the weak, weary and heavy-laden." Yogacharya always said they were his. He knew how to handle each one, for he was a pure channel of God with no ego. He gave of himself constantly and wholeheartedly and seemed to get his answers direct from God. When people left they were never the same, such was the depth of the blessings he bestowed on each and every one. He had a bubble of joy at all times, and he often kept us entertained with great stories and wonderful word pictures. He fascinated everyone.

There are hundreds of people who could likely write a book about their experiences with Yogacharya, so unique was this Blessed Soul who came to live among us for ninety-six years. For myself, I found his consciousness to be so vast, that I can only tell the world a very small portion, that small portion that he allowed me to perceive and experience. I believe I was blessed to be chosen to see that portion, because for years before ever meeting him I doggedly sought to know God better.

What I observed about him with the devotees was that he seemed to study and observe their needs, for he seemed to know their every thought. From the beginning and through the years, he built this organization based on the needs of the devotees who came to him. They were to be his lot in life. And so they came — at first hippies and flower children. The regular

Lecturing at the Ranch, 1972.

church goers moved on and the place soon became filled with the "weak, weary and heavy-laden" — and his mission began.

He never tried to fit them into a philosophy of life as he saw it. He listened and observed and through parables he caused them to take stock of themselves. He showed them how to build their self-esteem and live life to manifest their full potential, fulfill their heart's desire, and become what they set their mind to become, be it marriage, business, or just to live life harmoniously. He accomplished this for those who lived at his retreat by putting them in positions where they would grow best. He called daily life "the cement mixer," and so by the involvement of devotees and residents with each other, the edges were made smooth. They would find out what worked and what didn't work. He gave everyone that opportunity to find out. He was a mirror of each person's shortcomings. Those who were critical he criticized, those who were arrogant found him arrogant. But for the vast majority he gave unconditional love and friendship — a love so deep that everyone soon discovered they could do almost anything their heart desired, and it would come to pass in due time. If their desires were not good, they suffered the consequences and learned from them as well. Then they went back to their lives, being better for that experience of living at Yogacharya's retreat for a few years and having the kinks removed. He never attempted to set up an organization really. And in fact each time it grew to a good state, he seemingly sent people on their way, back into the world to test their new skills of right living and to become strong warriors in the battle of life.

In the average spiritual community there are sets of rules and structured behavior, but Yogacharya believed in as few rules as possible: No drinking, drugs, or smoking. He said everyone knew when they were

21

going wrong, so he allowed them to go wrong if it was necessary to learn a point. As a consequence, everyone around him had to learn to tolerate everyone else and their shortcomings. Thus they learned to let go, be tolerant, be peaceful, loving, and harmonious. He never told people how they should act or live. He'd let them find that out for themselves. He made rules as he went along, according to which individual he was dealing with. The first group were not allowed to leave the grounds except for two who did weekly shopping and errands (for which they took turns). At first he led the services at night, and he always expected everyone to attend. Eventually he had the devotees take turns leading the services. He expected the services to begin with prayers and they had to be perfect. He ruled like a loving father and was always a flawless example of love, tolerance, patience, and all God's qualities. His children were eager to please and tried to become like him. As the years went on he allowed for more freedom. People came and went a little more freely as the need arose. Since he knew their thoughts, the devotees worked at towing the line, each at his own speed and ability. He seldom criticized but let everyone get away with much. If a devotee took advantage and did not have a desire to improve, that devotee would eventually find himself on the outside. This was brought about in a subtle way, known perhaps only to the devotee. But he could and would be harsh if the situation warranted it.

Yogacharya's attitude toward monastery living was middle-of-the-line thinking, as was everything else. Since he had little or no ego, God seemingly came through him in an almost perfect flow. Life is a schoolroom of obstacles and so we either grow with the punches or we stay in the same grade until we learn that particular lesson. The better the person could listen, the faster the progress. Both the monastery and life in the fast lane, in "the cement mixer," as Yogacharya liked to call it, had their obstacles, the choice is ours. Yogacharya gave subtle help to whatever choice one made — sometimes not so subtle. He gave that help to monks who visited as well. It so happened that the first monk who came to the meditation group in Chicago in 1960 saw Yogacharya as an ordinary man controlled by the women admirers who swarmed around him and by his great wealth (for he was known to be quite wealthy upon his retirement from the auto parts manufacturing business). But neither was true, as time alone revealed.

The next two monks who came to visit Detroit a few years later were likely influenced by that first monk, for they didn't really know him either. They seemed to believe that women were Yogacharya's object. Since Yogacharya was a mirror of everyone who stood before him, and because he was a mirror of their thoughts, he completely convinced them that truly it was so. On this occasion, he sat with the devotees for fellowship, as was his habit each week after the Sunday service in Detroit. He had the two monks seated on either side of him. On this occasion everyone crowded around him. He was an enigma of joy and laughter. His inner bubble of love and happiness was felt by all. Though he was usually a little more remote, this time he showed the women devotees much attention, and when he got up to leave he even planted a kiss on the cheek of each of those standing behind his chair, much to the delight and surprise of the five or six of us standing there. The two monks were completely convinced that they were right, this was the lifestyle of Yogacharya! But the truth was that we, the women around him, were as shocked as were the monks. Such was the way he mirrored the thoughts of others, and in this case, the two monks who needed that lesson. Ordinarily, Yogacharya held all women at arm's length. In fact, all people could feel the remoteness — the inner man was never known to us.

On another occasion, a monk visited the ranch, Yogacharya's yoga retreat in northern Michigan. At that time, he used to hold Sunday services in a large room in the lodge. There was an organ in the middle of the room, and on that particular Sunday, the visiting monk sat down to play for the Sunday service. But unknown to him, there were two or three keys on that organ which could not be played. The regular organist just avoided them and played around them, and it was never noticed by anyone. Yogacharya had a playful expression on his face as he let the young man raise his hands and arms high in the air, lost in his music — lost too to the disaster just ahead! Such was the way he knocked the spiritual ego of people, bringing them down to a state of humility. Likely coming up against a teacher such as Yogacharya was the only way advanced spiritual souls such as the monks would get a needed lesson.

Yogacharya said spiritual egotism was the last thing to go, and I truly believe that. At times Yogacharya would come into the large room at the ranch where everyone was seated and he'd go into an act. He would fold his hands as in prayer arid pretend to look so very spiritual and then closing his eyes he would say in a voice of pretense, "Oh, I'm sooo spiritual," as he'd look heavenward. This act never failed to bring us all down to reality and each one would wonder, did he mean me? He took a crack at everyone's spiritual egotism, before it even could get a hold. Such was the depth of his inner subtle teaching.

Another monk came to visit the ranch, but I was not there at the time. That particular young man had all kinds of opinions and judgments of long and deep standing. If Yogacharya thought a person needed to be straightened out, even monks, he could and would do that in no uncertain terms. I'm told that took place, much to the young man's surprise and shock — so much so that the young man had to go lie down with a headache. As Yogacharya one day told me, a few days after meeting him, where I, years later, chided him over his "telling me off," he said, "Likely the first time anyone ever died." So with this young enthusiastic monk: "likely the first time anyone ever died." That's the chance they took when they came to Yogacharya's retreat to visit. You always remembered him when you went away!

After Yogacharya's death, the first monk with many "judgments and opinions" came back. He still expressed that he knew Yogacharya — something that none of us could really say, for he was unable to be known, in actuality. Others, too, came to visit, but they, too, only had opinions and judgments. None could really know. There was one, however, who knew and loved Yogacharya before he became a monk. He knew him as well as we did. In that particular man, there were no judgments and opinions, and so unconditional love poured through him to all of us who felt the loss of Yogacharya so very much. He alone of all the monks whom I knew who visited was a channel of that divine love which was the expression of the pure soul of Yogacharya Oliver.

Yogacharya was a teacher, but more by being a presence and an experience than by what he taught by word of mouth. From the moment you discovered him, he was a subtle glow in your heart. Devotees flocked around him like bees around honey, never exactly knowing what attracted them but drawn like iron filings to a magnet, People's problems disappeared in his presence, and questions got answered — such was the attraction of divine love. He lived it, he was divine love in human form. He taught by telling stories often humorous and enlightening, revealing that he knew all about everyone and their problems. Nothing was a secret before him. He seemed to have access to the most remote recesses of your mind.

When I first met him, he soon revealed to me that there was nothing hidden to him. He seemed to know my every motive, my every prayer and intention. My life was like an open book to him. When, you visited, you would bask in his great love, and when you left, you would go with great yearning to stay and with a desire to know him better expressing itself in your heart. You could never forget him, for you had been permanently touched. The Indians call it a "darshan." It left you with a desire to know God better, to be a better person, and with the inspiration to grow and make changes in your life, from that day forth. In many devotees, that divine seed was placed in them to take root sometime in the future. In some, it caused them to enter a spiritual path that was uncovered from some deep recess. They may never see him again, but the seed was planted on one of the many paths to God. He directed everyone on their own path or bent. Others might come back once a year, or once a month, but they would never be quite the same. They would seek in a spiritual direction, known only to them and God, but ever onward toward the light. There were others whom he drew toward him and toward his path of yoga, union with God.

Most devotees who found their way to him had great potential but were unable to manifest that potential. He built up the ego in most, for although the spiritual path was seemingly a path to overcome ego, it nevertheless had to be overcome from strength and not out of weakness. Building people was a lifetime process and he knew exactly how to do that for each one who came to him. He'd create a whole experience to enable that soul to unfold and develop and become what he knew it could become, what they themselves desired to become — ever upward and onward — any path, as long as it was Godward toward the light.

It took time for me to see Yogacharya as the pure channel that he was, a channel for God with his ego-self pushed aside, completely controlled. He was completely able to let God manifest through him with no will of his own. Especially was that apparent in his later years. Even from early on, he described himself as being like a pipe — that he had no powers of his own — the power came through him, he was just an instrument, he said.

Chapter 3 – Learning to Love

EARLY ON, HE SAID I WAS TOP OF THE CLASS.
But he also said I didn't even know what love was — in
answer to my question about loving someone. So, from
there on, I would practice love and forgiveness in
response to every lack of harmony with him or with
anyone else. I would form affirmations — loving all
those I found hard to love — thus, I felt in this way I
was building my love "muscles."

In one of the books by the spiritual author
Annalee Skarin, she urged us to send out love
vibrations. I had been trying to send out love vibrations
all these years (such as I defined love) and I wasn't
aware that it was anything special, except that I knew I
wanted to respond to Yogacharya's guidance and
teachings. I just thought by loving the least loveable, I
would automatically love the highest that I could and so
grow in my ability to love.

Annalee Skarin also reveals that it is the ability
to love which makes man a son of God. When I first got
interested in Christ and God, I reasoned that if I could
love as Jesus loved, I would likely have the power of
Jesus, and so, even as a small child, I attempted to love,
but soon found out that it is a horrendous thing to
attempt! Nevertheless, this thought was always in the
back of my mind. Yogacharya was aware from the
beginning of this desire of mine to learn to love. From
the early years when I met Yogacharya, he would bring
me to a place of great love for him. Then he would lead
me to an experience which would bring out great hate in

me. When it happened for the first time, I was so utterly shocked I thought my nervous system would never recover. We are capable of great resilience, so eventually I got over my hatred, intuitively realizing I had to learn to love, I had to be able to forgive and overcome this hatred — hatred which I did not know I was capable of feeling. After several months and many love affirmations and much work on myself, I did manage to forgive and forget about that particular incident.

Though Yogacharya taught many through dreams, I didn't usually have those experiences. But I do recall that I had one other very intense hate experience, and it was in a dream. It was so real that I woke up with a start, very shaken. I wondered what it was all about. In this dream I was sitting on a floor and was vehemently shouting, "1 hate you" to a man who was standing there. Somehow I knew he had all power over me. Even though I shouted "I hate you" over and over again, he said nothing. I awakened from this dream with a great start. Although this man was not Yogacharya, I knew he represented him, I knew too that it was a test to see how much I was overcoming my hatred. I never had any other intense experiences of hatred like those two. But I worked very hard after that to keep love uppermost, an unconditional, all-encompassing love for everyone, especially for those for whom I found myself having negative feelings, or anyone with whom I had any lack of harmony. I now know, upon reflecting back, that this was likely my first seed of love planted deep down in my consciousness and it replaced my deep-seated hatreds. I recognized that Yogacharya knew of my early childhood determination to love as Jesus loved, and so my growth pattern to love began to develop, under his tutelage.

Through the years Yogacharya would lead me to that place of hatred over and over again, but none were as shocking as that first time, when I doubted if I'd ever recover. But I now know, because I did recover, that I had a consciousness (and all of us have it) that was strengthened by the tests administered by my fabulous teacher who was able to give me the strength to recover. As the years went on, these points of hatred became less powerful and my ability to overcome them became easier. I learned ever-greater love and forgiveness and even to forget all negative emotions. It is no wonder, Yogacharya told me (when he first met me) that I did not know the real meaning of love. I know now that I did not. Another time he also told me that love and hate were the same. I have yet to learn to understand that, but I expect to have that realization someday.

Throughout 35 years there were so many occasions when he did things that would arouse hatred in me; and always I would respond by developing ever-greater love and forgiveness. I worked constantly on myself — upon every negative reaction. He taught everyone according to their own understanding. I always understood exactly what he was doing with me. I never did get to the place where I could respond with love at the time of each adversity. It always took a while. But in his subtle way of teaching, he showed me how it had to be done. His teaching was never in words, and so I was usually shown by an experience — that experience came one day in the form of a young man who suddenly appeared from nowhere. He was 23 years of age, but I immediately recognized that he was a very old soul and had the maturity of a much older man, with an advanced state of spirituality. Many were to learn much from this young man in the next few years, when he joined the staff of the ranch.

For me, the lesson I learned was when Yogacharya suddenly told this young man to leave. The young man showed much distress over this, but when Yogacharya's car drove up to the door and we all ran out to greet him, it was this same young man who opened the car door and addressed Yogacharya very sweetly and lovingly, "Would you like a cup of coffee, Yogacharya?" Recognition of this young man's capability of instant love and forgiveness didn't miss me, who was looking on. I thought to myself at the time, I wish I could love, forgive and forget like that!

Sometime later, it happened that this same young man was pumping gas at a nearby gas station when I drove up. As I walked toward him, he looked up and said to me, "I love you, too." He was indeed an experience! It must be 25 years since I last saw him. I can't help wondering where he must be on the spiritual path at this point in time. I believe people regularly cross your path to teach you something. Learning to love as Yogacharya loved became an obsession with me and still is. It is always in the background of my mind and the reason for my very existence. Yogacharya was always a mystery to me and likely everyone else as well, for he was our favorite topic of conversation. We never stopped marveling at the things he did and everything he knew about us all.

The Cement Mixer

Ten days before Yogacharya left us, he sent me away for the third time. I knew I always did better in the "cement mixer," as he called life outside of the ranch. I still needed the adversity. I was devastated, but when he shocked us by leaving his body, I did settle down, more so after feeling his loving presence in Chicago.

All along my spiritual climb, I would come across books that were exactly right for me at the time. The I AM books were one group that seemed to be speaking to me. I read every one of them several times, as was my habit, absorbing everything. I read them years ago. They spoke of experiences that were the same as I was experiencing at the time. I was very enthused and inspired by the I AM books. I reread them for years. I felt like a sponge soaking up spring water. These books were the wellspring. I never knew where their saints fit in the overall scheme of things, I only knew I felt that they did fit. I'd feel a Presence when I'd pick the books up. I loved every one of them. I intuitively knew Yogacharya had led me to the first one I read. It was number 2 of 8 volumes. There was a similarity to the five books entitled, *The Life and Teachings of the Masters of the Far East.* When they talked of the ascended masters and the White Brotherhood, (white meaning "light") I truly believed there was such a society of saintly souls. On more than one occasion, Yogacharya admitted to belonging to the White Brotherhood. I took the first two of the I AM books to the ranch, where Yogacharya approved of my giving them to the devotees there. They, too, became engrossed.

After Yogacharya left the body, I again became involved with books — this time a group of books by Annalee Skarin. She was a very devout Mormon whom the Mormons were unable to believe when she said that God had told her to write these books. They excommunicated her from the Mormon Church. Yogacharya encouraged people to read these books, but I had never come across them until one day when the present director of the ranch, Bob Raymer, started a bookstore and stocked all eight titles on the shelves. After reading the first one, *Ye Are Gods*, I once more recaptured a sense of spiritual exultation and inspiration. Like the I AM books, these books spoke to my very soul. The author began by discussing a saying of Jesus, "The things I do, if you believe, you also shall do, and greater things than this shall you do." This was the statement that had started me on my spiritual journey when I first arrived in Chicago, and now re-invoked my spiritual quest. I must confess, after Yogacharya left the body, I had put things on the back burner for a while, so to speak. This great spiritual truth contained in Jesus' promise to his followers, "greater than this shall you do," is not something that I have ever heard discussed by the mainstream Christian community, even though I tune my radio to Christian broadcasts every day, both at home and while I'm driving in my car.

Annalee's books made me feel alive once again, after Yogacharya's departure, for I began to understand how he became the spiritual giant that he was. She declares that her books are the further teachings of Christ for which he said people were not ready at the time he lived on the earth. In *Ye Are Gods* she maintains that no man is greater than his power to humble himself.

Yogacharya one day looked into my eyes and in a very serious tone of voice he said to me, "Humility is the key to power, just remember that." I had got that message firmly planted in my consciousness from the many times he kept hammering away at my ego.

Annalee said the seed of God is in every man, and as love is perfected, the seed grows. I know that Yogacharya helped that seed to start growing in me in his subtle way, as he did with everyone. He helped me to fulfill my spiritual aspirations. For everyone who came to him, I saw the same pattern was there — he helped them to fulfill their potential, whether it was to find a good marriage, to join the monastic path, simply to gain confidence and self-esteem, or to find the meaning of loving as Jesus loved. This latter was and is my goal. To grow in love, one has to overcome hatred and negative emotions. I have a long way to go on my chosen path, but I feel he has caused me to overcome a deep-seated hatred of which I wasn't aware. One can't truly grow in divine love until hatred is overcome.

Reading Annalee Skarin's books gave me a fantastic insight into the mystique of the life of Yogacharya and also his treatment of me. For one thing she talks about the preparedness of the soul. I who hardly said one prayer in my early years did however aim at perfection. Prior to Yogacharya coming into my life I communed with God for about eight years. I called it meditation, hut it really was not. I would read the Unity Church's "Daily Word" and other publications. I would talk to God and form affirmations in order to change my wrong thinking. Thus I developed an intense desire to achieve knowing God better. As Annalee

Skarin says, "An intensity of the desire to achieve is the controlling factor." I immediately felt she was right, for I notice many who have an intense desire to achieve perfection. The great basketball player Michael Jordan is one of them. I don't know if he takes God as his partner, but for those who do, I notice they go up, up and up continually. Oprah attempts to take God as her partner. She has had many programs which reveal this factor. And recently I've been reading *Prayer, My Adventure with God*, by Robert Schuller. I marvel at such a life as I read it and I believe it absolutely. For although Yogacharya didn't have the desires of Robert Schuller, there are parallels. I once read a book about Mother Teresa and she too, because she lived God's laws, the laws of the universe, would automatically have everything come to her, filling her needs as she went along.

Since Yogacharya was my teacher assigned by God (I was told in a meditation that he was my Guru, at a time when I did not know what a guru truly was), I follow his perfect example. That example is also outlined in Annalee Skarin's books. The Bible says it well by James, apostle of Jesus: "My brethren count it all joy when you fall into divine temptations — knowing that the trying of your faith worketh patience. But let patience have its perfect work that ye may be perfect and whole, wanting nothing." In the book *As a Man Thinketh* by James Allen, he writes: "Man is buffeted by circumstances so long as he believes himself to be the creature of outside conditions, but when he realizes that he is a creature of power and that he may command the hidden soul and seed of his being out of which circumstance grows, he then becomes the rightful master of himself."

I interpret that as meaning if you can determine the laws of the universe, God's laws, and live by them every minute, you can achieve, or become, whatever you desire. Just as I had seen in an inner vision before I ever came to Chicago when I saw a line which I knew to be myself and I saw circles which were thoughts surrounding that line and then I was given the interpretation as expressed above. These things gave me a clue as to how Yogacharya became the divine master I knew him to be.

Chapter 4 – An Angel in Disguise

YOGACHARYA HAD A GREAT ABILITY to hide his fantastic consciousness when it was needed to be hidden, such as when he was teaching me when I first met him. One day when I'd come, I'd feel this divine Presence which he was, another day I'd come and he would seem like a different man, an ordinary human being. After going through this experience a few times, I concluded he was a divine actor on the stage of life. His actions were entirely for the Divine Director, God. It was through this ability he had to bond with me that eventually I would feel his presence in mine, leading me and teaching me every step of the way. He was so at one with God that I would always know when I'd gone wrong in my thoughts or motives, for his Presence would be gone, until I would right my thinking — much as one feels a sense of conscience — God's consciousness in us.

When he hosted banquets twice a year in Detroit for the sake of Detroit members, I was there, the first one from Chicago. I felt such a fantastic consciousness of love emanating from Yogacharya that I had a hard time leaving when it was time to go. Ever after that, I encountered one obstacle after another as I attempted to return to the Detroit banquets. After a while, I got the message — they weren't for me. I reasoned since the Detroit banquets weren't meant for me and I wasn't welcome, I decided I'd organize one for Chicago. It wasn't difficult to get people to pay $35 a plate for a dinner to benefit the ranch if they had once met Yogacharya. Consequently, I was able to get 49 people together, and we set up the date. Yogacharya never implied to me that he did not want us in Chicago to do this. He came to the Chicago banquet, and it was a huge success — people loved to be near him, that is to say, for everyone except me. For me the whole thing was a great obstacle course – the man who was to be the emcee arrived about 15 minutes before it was to begin. Yogacharya himself arrived by plane, traveling with the woman who cared for him — I met them at the airport, and, as they walked off the plane, he seemed so different to me. It was as though he had completely turned off his fabulous consciousness. He appeared and acted like an ordinary man in every way. Now usually he exuded a consciousness to me that was very difficult to describe other than to say he radiated a divine aura — a divine magnetism. On the way to the banquet hall I was very worried, for I had sold $35 tickets to many people who had not met him but had heard about this divine magnetic soul and were eager to meet him! When we finally arrived, I was very greatly relieved to find that his consciousness radiated just as much love and magnetism as one could ever imagine, directed towards all the devotees that had gathered to hear him, and be near him. The evening was a great success for everyone but myself. They loved him and basked in his divine aura of joy, love and laughter, which he exhibited. They left feeling very joyful and satisfied. When I took Yogacharya and his companion who cared for him back to the plane, he remained completely turned off (the only way I can describe it) to me, acting the role of a tired, elderly man — very elderly, indeed.

Although this experience should have taught me something — that he did not want me to hold banquets in Chicago — it did not. I was determined to have another one the following year. His philosophy to me had always been "to let things happen — don't try to make them happen." This is what he'd say to me. Well, the following year, I was undaunted — I went all out to have a great banquet. The devotees got together to form a band to play beautiful yoga chants, and we had a singer whose voice was like a nightingale — all ready to sing his favorites.

When it was time for his plane to arrive, we suddenly got word that he was grounded — the plane was covered with ice, and he would not be able to make it! There were 49 people (again) who had paid $35 and were sitting around the banquet table waiting. I was in shock! As things turned out, even though Yogacharya wasn't able to make it, there were two beautiful young devotees who came forward. One of them emceed, while the other spoke of his experiences with Yogacharya. Both young men had wonderful, miraculous experiences to tell, and they were incredible. The very charming emcee then ended the program with a meditation which was so charged with the presence of Yogacharya that, when it was time to end, the people still remained seated, even though many of them had never meditated before the banquet event. They finally had to be dismissed. We all agreed that though Yogacharya was not there in the flesh, that his Presence shone through those two young men and entered the consciousness of everyone sitting there — a consciousness of love, peace, and joy, just as though Yogacharya had been there in person. It was a great evening, enjoyed by all. However,

I never again attempted to organize another banquet in Chicago for people to meet Yogacharya.

As Yogacharya neared the age of 90, he didn't seem to want to talk much anymore, or teach the newcomers who came to the Ranch. He would simply attend the evening meditations, often not talking to anyone. But, for those of us who knew him, we knew how blessed we were just to have him there — just to be in his presence. During this time, there were many people who would come and go who had heard of him. Many felt he was just an ordinary elderly man — nothing special — and he would respond like he wanted to convince them they were right — he was just an old man, nothing special.

But, when someone would arrived that he knew, who needed his guidance for whatever reason known only to Yogacharya, that person would become completely aware immediately that they were in the presence of a saint. I remember one young man who was there for a week. During this period, he would sit on the floor near Yogacharya during the evening meditation. When Yogacharya would leave, he'd get up and stand in the doorway watching Yogacharya until he was out of sight. After this young man left, he wrote to Yogacharya asking if he should come to live at the Ranch, or stay with his teacher, an Indian Yogi at whose ashram he had been living for eleven years (since the Yogi had founded his organization). Yogacharya replied that he should stay where he was. He usually guided people in their own chosen path. He never tried to change their individual bent. The young man said he had learned the importance of meditation and communing with God in his life.

Yogacharya allowed those of us whom he wanted to know only what he wanted each of us to know. He knew exactly what each one was to be taught. To those whom he did not want to be in awe of him, he could keep them from recognizing him completely. He had that power. He always said his work was done more on the astral planes than on this earthly plane.

One devotee who came to him and was thinking of leaving had gone to see a psychic in Toronto. The psychic told her she saw a great soul in her life. When the devotee admitted this was Yogacharya and that she was thinking of leaving, the psychic told her that she must not, that this was a great saint sent here, that he had much to do with this planet and much to do on the astral plane yet. This devotee then returned and stayed at the Ranch until Yogacharya left his body.

Such was the consciousness of this great soul. If you arrived on the grounds of the Ranch and you ran across Yogacharya, you might mistake him for a kindly old gardener, if that was as much as he wanted to reveal to you. He alone seemed to know what each one was to be taught and when they were to be sent away to be taught in the cement mixer — as he called the world outside of his Ranch. But it would seem that he was always with those who were blessed to have met him, whether they were aware or not, whether they stayed close or not. He was like an angel in disguise.

Chapter 5 – When the Darkness is Cast Out

ANNALEE SKARIN STATES in her book entitled *The Book of Books*, "Many have never accepted the dynamic challenge to LIVE Christ's teachings. Many think they are proving their belief by going forth and hammering others with their interpretations as they send forth their haranguements in discordant, sanctimonious self-righteousness. Yet Christ's actual teachings have never been acknowledged as a Way of Life and of fulfillment or an everlasting privilege of stupendous accomplishment crowned with every reward contained in every Promise ever given since time began."

She states further, "The First and Great Commandment, when lived, contains the breathtaking fulfillment of every promise God ever gave, plus all perfection and all power within. It is held forever the fulfilling of the love which brings into one's life a complete knowledge of the things which 'Eye hath never seen, nor ear heard,' neither hath entered into the heart of man — those unspeakable stories which God has prepared for those who love Him, and prove it by their living of the law pertaining to it."

Yogacharya reached that high spiritual level and proved to all who knew him who had aspirations to do the same. These things are proved in the experiences that were given to some of us that revealed that "eye hath not seen," indeed.

Before Yogacharya established a retreat in northern Michigan, two young devotees and I went to the ranch to be with Yogacharya for one weekend. A caretaker and his wife were the only other people on the grounds. In the afternoon, he had told my two young friends and me that he would take us to see his other property which was nearby. At the last minute, unexpectedly, he announced that we could not go. We resisted, but he was adamant — we could not go. So he left us alone on this 800 acres of woods. The caretaker was in a building at the bottom of the hill, and we were staying in a big lodge on the top of the hill.

We meditated and listened to tapes of Yogacharya's yoga services, given on Sundays at the Art Institute in Detroit. Around ten o'clock at night, when ordinarily it would be pitch black outside if there were no moon to light our way, we noticed that it was like daylight outside the lodge. We looked at our wristwatches to check the time. What could it be? We went outside to see what was causing this great light. Lo and behold, the sky looked like it consisted of millions of tiny stars blinking, lighting up the entire atmosphere. We were so awed by the sight, we ran down to the top of the boathouse and looked into the water, which appeared to have millions of tiny fireflies blinking up at us — on and off, on and off — in magical fashion. The sky appeared like it was so close we could almost reach up and touch it. The young girl looked up at this fabulous, magical sight and exclaimed, "Oh, he is with us anyway!" These two young people and I were the only ones who saw that miraculous scene.

When Yogacharya came back the following weekend and we excitedly told him what we had seen, he passed it off like he had nothing to do with it. He merely said casually, "Oh, we often have that kind of phenomena up here," as he strolled away.

Annalee Skarin expresses it thus: "As one masters the realms of darkness by learning to use the divine switch to turn on the Light, he becomes filled with Light, and the very realms of heaven become His to explore and to use, as all things in heaven, the elements, the glory and the power, become subject to Him. This subjection is but the ability to take hold of the elements of Light and Primal substance, or divine material, and mold it into form, useable and dynamic in its power of fulfilling." She further states, "These are the things of heaven that become subject unto one as he begins to make use of them. WHEN THE DARKNESS IS CAST OUT, He becomes glorious, according to the Promise or Covenant."

Yogacharya would tell people to read Annalee Skarin. Her books explain what I have experienced with Yogacharya. Our present spiritual director at the Ranch, Bob Raymer, started a bookstore and has all her books on the shelves. It wasn't until then that I started to read her books. He, too, like Yogacharya, knew they contained great truths. He, too, knows that "the things of earth" that become "subject unto one are the material things which he has developed the power to bring forth and fashion from that primal element."

I expect Yogacharya knew I would someday attempt to write a book about him and the marvel of his great consciousness, because I bought a recorder and left it at the Art Institute when Yogacharya held his services. One of the devotees there would record them for me every week. I would also attend his Thursday night services, after which he would take five of us and teach us his great wisdom as we sat around him at a restaurant until the wee hours of the morning. I was entranced and would write things down on scraps of paper. None of us knew how very blessed we were to have had these opportunities long ago (1959 or 60). The other four aren't part of his organization now (two are dead).

It is no wonder that I had a revelation as I got into writing this book to incorporate Annalee Skarin's teachings with the life of Yogacharya. Her writings take on an earthly form in Yogacharya. Annalee Skarin states that these gifts belong also to the one who "overcomes the evils of his life" as he brings forth "the desires of his own envisioning, holding steadfastly to his hope until it materializes and takes tangible form." She states, "This is the law and the Promise. The Primal matter becomes his to manipulate and to create with. This is the material reality of which a child's modeling clay is but a toy. And all things are possible to him who believes. For everyone who asks, receives."

Before the Ranch became the "Retreat of Excellence" that it is today (that was Yogacharya's name for it, those many years ago), I was there alone with a woman friend of mine. One evening, I was telling her how my mother would. take her four children on picnics and how we would all pick blueberries. I was six years younger than the next youngest of my sisters, so I wasn't a picker like they were, but I loved the experience of being in nature, with the berries, the sun, and the nearness of my family. I would experience a great ecstatic feeling of love and I described it!

The following day, she and I walked down a wonderful path at the ranch, an open area surrounded by trees. It was a beautiful day, sunny and warm. And, lo and behold, there were bushes of blueberries everywhere! We were thrilled as we picked and ate berries and communed with nature for several hours. I once again experienced that great ecstatic feeling of love, just as I had in my childhood setting, so many years ago. The next day was just as wonderful as the last, so my friend and I set out early, complete with pails, this time to gather and bring back the luscious fruit. When we arrived at the same spot, we searched and searched, but no blueberries were to be found anywhere. My friend seemed to know the explanation before I did. She turned to me and said, "You were given that experience, so much like the one of your childhood!" I then knew she was right, that that was a spiritual experience that I was blessed to be given by Yogacharya. There were no blueberries on the ranch property ever, before or since.

I met Yogacharya in 1959 when I had a great need and was seeking such a great soul to heal me and to guide me, so, when I was blessed to find him, I became aware of his great consciousness right away. However, nothing bonded me to him as much as this third experience which happened in those early years. I had left the ranch and Yogacharya one day early in the morning with my mother. We were bound for Chicago, a distance of nearly 400 miles. I was sleepy at the beginning, and I grew sleepier as we drove along. I stopped many times for coffee and breaks — anything and everything people suggested that might keep me awake. Finally, around 5 p.m., we arrived on the outer drive around Chicago. My mother said something to me, and, getting no response, she touched my arm. I awakened from an apparent deep sleep, looked around and saw I was driving alone, successfully, but surrounded by lanes of traffic on either side of me! My mother was so shocked and afraid as she saw how deep a sleep I had been in, she could only exclaim, "O Betty!" I quickly took stock of the situation and also quickly took over the control of my car from "whoever" was driving in my place! We reached home safely, but from that day forth, I've never been afraid when driving. To this day, nearly 40 years later, I guess I know, there's an angel who looks out for me, if I attempt to abide by the laws of the road and right living. By this bonding experience, I felt a security that I never felt before.

Chapter 6 – My Bubble of Joy

JESUS HAD SAID when he lived on earth that he had much more to teach, but that men of His time were not ready for it. Annalee Skarin came with further words of Jesus, but apparently the Mormons were not ready for them, for they excommunicated her. She said the books she had written were from Christ and in the *Book of Books* — her last book of eight — she quotes from the Bible, "In Him we live, move and have our being." Then she compares it to the earthly fact that an embryonic infant in the mother's womb has its being in her. It lives and moves in her, but it is not her, and the mother is not it. She then says we do not realize that we are held in Light and Spirit until we become fully formed as sons and daughters of God — evolved into perfection. This is the eternal truth that man must begin to comprehend.

Yogacharya used to tell us a little story about fishes. He said, one day all the little fishes went to see the wise fish in order to hear what water was. The wise fish told them they lived and moved and had their being in it. The little fishes then went back to their homes and talked it over, and decided they still didn't know what water was. Then Yogacharya would laugh and laugh, as he would lovingly look at our puzzled expressions, for we, too, were not ready for these great words of wisdom.

But for those of us who were blessed to have experienced this divine soul amongst us, so much more divine than human — but both human and divine — we know that the things written by Annalee Skarin are absolute truths, for we were privileged to perceive them in Yogacharya. I myself saw it in his luminous face and glowing eyes when I first met him, and I saw it:

- In the experience of his changing into light before my very eyes, while at the same lime I was experiencing a strange power almost forcing me to prostrate at his feet — then his changing back to himself before it could happen.

- In his fantastic ability to know the thoughts of all of us around him and to point each one in the direction he should go.

- In his ability to perceive our life situations — seemingly all at the same time.

- In his glorious divine love that at times was so great that there are no words to describe it.

- In his magnetic Presence, which was irresistible at the times when it was needed.

- In his aura of peace, which was a cure-all for those who manifested the consciousness of darkness and depression and who found their way to him.

- In his ability to draw a mental line to keep back a person whom he felt should be held back, preventing that person from getting any closer to him.

- In his life-changing inspiration which reached out to all who were ready and desiring to know God better.

- In his miraculous touch when that was what was needed.

- In his ability to bond with every devotee who wanted his love and direction, and then to withdraw his consciousness when need be, to teach the way of perfection and purity.

- In his ability to come to people in visions, in dreams, and even transport his physical body in order to lift or teach devotees the next step up the spiritual ladder.

- In his complete control of his eyes in an unblinking state for hours at a time (as I observed at a Kriya service).

- In his ability to know devotees better than they knew themselves: their past and events in their future, and their exact bent.

- In his ability to teach anyone who came to him with a problem how to solve it — be it health, business, or the next step up the spiritual ladder.

- In his ability to cause one to feel secure "in his presence," even when far away from him.

- In his unique ability to always be that great presence of joy and love, and be able to give it to all absolutely unaffected by any number of negative people around him. His powerful consciousness would change their darkness into joy and happiness.

- In his ability to know our weaknesses and strengths — like a mirror — often even before we stood before him.

- In his ability to come through people when necessary.

- In his ability to go with little or no sleep and his need for very little food.

- In his ability to seemingly know everything in one's life and give the right answers to each and every problem.

- In his ability to never take responsibility for conditions around him — being able to completely let go of everything and let God come through him for his answers.

- In his ability to just be the answer for everyone who sought him — the weak, weary, and heavy-laden, who found their way to him from all walks of life and from all ends of the world: India, Germany, Mexico, and all over the U.S.A. and Canada.

He was indeed an angel among us and seemed to be omniscient, omnipresent, and omnipotent.

Annalee Skarin expressed it well when she said that as one learns to love God with all one's heart, mind, soul, and strength — he will become filled with light and comprehend all things and will be born of the spirit. He will become "evolved from the worm state of grubby mortality."

She further states that this is symbolic of man evolving into his own perfection — and that joy is the spiritual condition of perfection — a joy that cannot possibly be understood — it is not hilarity — it is an entirely spiritual condition belonging to those who overcome. She says joy is of the saints and none else can put it on, but they alone. Yogacharya often would say, "I always have my bubble of joy right here," and he'd point to his heart. He would encourage us to keep on so that when we get enough in our spiritual bank account, we too would really know God.

He was the greatest example, greatest channel, and greatest manifestation of what God can do when man knocks, seeks, and finds long enough. It can't be achieved overnight, but by persistent effort and belief. Each person must work upon himself, not others.

Annalee Skarin says we must become masters of our own thoughts, emotions, and inclinations — and purify ourselves with the giving of love. She says it is time for man to rise and soar into the higher realms, and to begin to do the greater works of which Christ spoke. Works that have never seemed possible before, even though we have always had the equipment.

We, too, every one of us, can reach this tremendous level of perfection that this blessed soul had reached. We too can be an angel here on earth, so very greatly needed in this day of darkness. It will likely be the only way that we can turn back the clock. We must ask, seek, and knock, and develop greater thirst and hunger for perfection in all we do. There are many who think they have it all, when in actuality they really have only a little. They accept what men tell them instead of listening to God and becoming ever more desirous to know more and more of God.

I heard a minister say recently that our goal is to live in God's glory, but I feel our goal is to ask, seek, and knock until we know God better and reach the level of this blessed soul who demonstrated that it can be done. Isaiah 28 records it thus, precept upon precept — here a little, there a little.

Yogacharya's greatest ability perhaps was how by his great selfless love and divine friendship he would turn people away from living for themselves and doing things from their egos into being ever greater channels of God — living for God alone. And thus they would find out how much happier they became and how much more successful in life, and how much more fulfilled, as their ego-self was forgotten and cast aside for the greater glory of God.

And when he left us, we could still feel that guiding presence, showing us the way, as we would go within and listen to the inner voice. We might call that inner voice, God, Christ, or guru, it matters not, for we found out it is all the same. I and God are one, and to the degree we can let God live through us, we can be an ever greater channel.

The Bible says nothing is impossible to him who believes, "Eye hath not seen, and ear hath not heard." And God's promises must be fulfilled. We must lay hold of the best gifts. The Bible further says, "He who is thankful in all things shall be made glorious, and the things of the earth shall be added unto him one hundredfold, yea, more." The very vibrations of gratitude and appreciation place one in tune with the divine.

We are told we shall have dominion over all conditions and circumstances, if we live by God's promises. The birds and the animals shall be at our command as we learn to bring our own physical being into subjection, obeying the laws of God.

One day, as Yogacharya drove to a farm, all the cows came over and licked his car (he had to have it washed for the service the next day!). As he walked by the bank of the river, a little otter swam alongside of him until he reached the house. So very often, those of us who were around him, saw evidence of the divine level of consciousness to which one can evolve.

According to Annalee Skarin, "God says he who prays continually without ceasing shall have his mind opened to comprehend my mysteries. And unto him will be given the power to comprehend all things, and he will be given power to reveal things which have never been revealed and bring thousands of souls unto repentance or unto knowledge of my powers centered in their own souls." The nearer you approach perfection, the clearer will be your views and the greater will be your enjoyments until you overcome the evils of your life, the darkness, the doubting, the self-righteousness and all mortal negations, until one becomes truly born of the spirit.

God says all He has is ours. We must ask and we will receive, seek and we will find, knock and it will be opened unto us. Nothing is impossible to him who believes.

Joy is of the saints and none but they can put it on, but they alone.

Love is of the elect and none can receive it fully except you who have been developing it within you from the beginning.

So great was the love and joy of the divine and aura of eternal bliss around Yogacharya, that for those of us blessed to be present and know his indescribable peace, we will never, never forget — nor does a day ever pass that he is not in our thoughts or in our consciousness.

In the *Autobiography of a Yogi* by Paramahansa Yogananda, he refers to another saint who said, "Win conviction of God's Presence through your own joyous communion in meditation."

And the Bible says, "If your eyes be single to my glory, your whole body shall be filled with Light. And that body which is filled with Light shall comprehend all things. And the two greatest of all laws when lived, will fulfill all other laws."

And Annalee Skarin states Christ does not travel this path for any individual or group of individuals. Each must travel it for Christ, for when He appears, we are to be like Him. We are to purify ourselves even as He is pure. And it is up to each individual to sanctify his own life. This is the only way man can truly glorify God as he fulfills "His Words and Promises" and returns them unto Him completed — himself — glorified. Christ truly did the works of "overcoming" as He traveled the road in its most difficult aspects, alone and without precedent.

The first step upon this Straight and Narrow Path of purification is begun when one opens his mind and heart and soul in a desire to fulfill and live by those two first and great Commandments of Love. To actually live them is much more than just accepting them as Christ's sayings. It means to make them a living part of one's life.

Christ said, "Live the laws and you will know." MAN HAS NEVER ACCEPTED THE DYNAMIC CHALLENGE, TO LIVE CHRIST'S TEACHING. One will certainly know when one has reached this level in God's great outpouring of love. "Your mind and lips will have lost their power to hurt or wound and your voice will be heard among the Gods." Having seen Yogacharya live this, before our very eyes, makes the above words come alive. Thus, we all would become inspired to become a saint like he was. In this world of today, saints are badly needed. And it is possible for all of us to reach that level of the saints!

Chapter 7 – Just A Divine Show

I ORIGINALLY GOT INTERESTED in yoga through the wonderful pure teaching of Paramahansa Yogananda and the book of his life, *Autobiography of a Yogi*. His philosophy was based mostly on meditation and listening to God. Before he left this world, he established his organization, Self-Realization Fellowship, in California. Yogacharya Oliver conducted Self-Realization Fellowship meetings in Detroit, holding weekly services in the Detroit Art Institute. Yogacharya was Yogananda's oldest living disciple, and he followed his guru's precepts in everything. He read Yogananda's weekly sermons at the Sunday services, allowed only Yogananda's chants to be sung, (original compositions by Yogananda and Indian chants which Yogananda had translated into English).

When Yogacharya founded Song of the Morning Ranch in Vanderbilt, Michigan, he established a retreat there where SRF services were held and Yogananda's chants were sung, just as in Detroit. The retreat also held a quiet nightly meditation service, after which Yogacharya taught everyone who came to him. Yogananda bestowed the title of Yogacharya on him in 1951. Yogacharya means teacher of yoga, and, indeed, he was that — the best that one could have been blessed to have had.

At the retreat Yogacharya founded in 1970, he established these standards which are followed to this day:

- To practice and teach the use of meditation as a tool that people can use to uncover their true Inner Self and reach their Divine potential. The belief is that meditation is the quickest route to full realization of the Self.

- To teach a variety of yoga disciplines in a practical, science-based way so that people can develop a better understanding of their physical, mental, and spiritual potential.

- To explore, compare, and teach, not only the philosophy of yoga, but all philosophies that serve to improve humankind, and create a better environment in which people can reach their highest potential.

- To encourage the study of comparative religion, philosophy, and science,

- To investigate unexplained laws of nature and the powers latent in human beings.

- To provide people with opportunities and facilities to reach a better understanding of themselves, their environment, the universe, and God on an interdenominational, interfaith, and international scope.

Yogacharya meditating at the Ranch, 1975.

Perhaps it was because of these very free-flowing ideals of Yogacharya, or perhaps it was because he was so outgoing and taught all of us to be the same, that we learned to put the other person first, us second. He taught us selflessness by his very example at all times. That approach to God differed from the SRF approach of silence, silence, silence. We never stopped talking around Yogacharya except to listen to his teachings and his wonderful teaching stories with his great ability to use word pictures. He kept us entertained almost all of the time. But we did practice silence every night for 45 minutes and longer at special meditations.

I had an SRF meditation group in Chicago which met at my apartment for 12 years. We followed the SRF instructions of how it was to be conducted. The devotees arrived in silence; we meditated for 45 minutes, and then the devotees left in silence.

When I began to notice that the SRF monks looked on Yogacharya differently than we did, I became a little offended. I felt pulled in two different directions — one, SRF, and the other, Yogacharya's organization, Golden Lotus. Finally, I went to the Mother Center in California where SRF has its yearly convocation.

By the time I arrived, I had worked myself up into a real state of rebellion and resistance to the monks. I knew Yogacharya was pure, as also the teachings of Yogananda, so I wanted a sign from Yogananda that Yogacharya and Daya Mata, the President of SRF, were one and the same. At that time, around 1969-70, SRF was not as large as at the present time, so they began by taking the leaders of the meditation groups on a tour around the Headquarters. I can't recall exactly how it happened that I was taken, all alone, to see Yogananda's former bedroom by a nun of the order, but there I was, alone, and so very engrossed in what I wanted to say to Yogananda. His shoes were peeking out from under the bed. In my mind, I was addressing Yogananda as if he were standing in them. I was so preoccupied and focused on telling him about his monks and how unhappy I was with them, and how I couldn't continue to hold SRF group meetings in my home any longer that I didn't even notice that there were no other devotees around, just myself.

When I finally finished what I had to say (in my mind), a nun appeared in the room, (or perhaps she had been standing there the entire time). The nun then led me to the next room, where Daya Mata was sitting. I must have looked upset; I certainly felt like an enraged bull. Daya Mata put out her hands to me, and I completely melted as I put my hands in hers. Her glowing countenance and radiance stopped me in my tracks. And then, she whispered one word to me: "Peace." Her eyes had an expression with which I was very familiar, for I had seen that laughing expression in the eyes of Yogacharya many times, when I'd become adamant about something. In a glance, his eyes would say, "Don't take life so seriously, it is just a divine show." My troubles instantly went away, and I became miraculously peaceful. The nun then led me to the chapel, where, once more, I found I was still alone.

I sat in the middle of the chapel all by myself. I gazed at the painting of Yogananda which hung at the right side of the altar — one which was painted by a devotee who never knew him. It was beautiful and exactly like the photograph of his last smile. Suddenly, as I looked at it, streaks of light came out from the picture all around it. I blinked my eyes to see if I was seeing things or not. But the light streaks stayed there. At the same time, I experienced a great welling up of tears. I sobbed as if I would never stop. I had had the same experience at the mausoleum where Yogananda's body was kept. For me, it was a very embarrassing experience, but at both times it came on suddenly and I was unable to stop it. Fortunately for me at this time, there was no one in the chapel but myself. This experience finally ended just as abruptly as it had come, and before the chapel filled up with people. When I left the service, I had such a high consciousness and lightness, it seemed like my feet weren't touching the ground. I didn't want to say one thing to anyone or have anyone talk to me, for I knew I would lose it at the first contact. I never had an experience so high before or

Betty, Daya Mata, and another devotee, 1975.

since. I truly was given a sign! When I later saw the young monks, I had an overwhelming feeling of love and a desire to hug them — a nurturing, mothering feeling. All was forgiven and forgotten. I knew that Daya Mata and Yogacharya were one, and so I went on holding the SRF meditation group meetings at my home for many more years, always knowing that appearances are often deceiving.

Chapter 8 – Ever Greater Joy to All

I INTUITIVELY HAD ALWAYS BELIEVED Jesus to have been a wayshower. He showed us how to overcome the grades of life which took many incarnations, evolving all the way from the caveman state of being, to His state, that of Christ consciousness. He told us to seek, knock and find, and that if we worked at overcoming and loving, as he had done, the way would be opened to us. Someday we would, in some incarnation, reach a stage of evolution where we too, would be perfect sons of God — for He said, "The things I do, if you believe, you also can do, and greater things than this shall you do." I've never been able to forget these words of Jesus, the Christ. Seeing and knowing Yogacharya and experiencing his divine love convinced me that perfection could be attained. But it required effort — to practice, practice, practice, learning to love — the kind of love needed to cast out fears and negation, doubts, and evils. And, for some people, many, many lifetimes, many, many grades in the school of life. Love that does nothing is like sounding brass and clashing cymbals. When a man interviewed on television told of his two episodes of dying and coming back and when he said he learned in the experience that everything he had done in his lifetimes had to be paid for, (karma, yoga calls it) I understood what Yogacharya meant when he taught that we pay for every "jot and tittle," even every wrong thought. It will take many incarnations to arrive at the high state which Yogacharya had reached.

Yogacharya said there were many dimensions above us. Christ said, "There are many mansions in God's house." The Bible says we have to love God with all our heart, soul, mind, and strength, and love our neighbor as ourselves. Yogacharya was love incarnate. He lived and radiated it to everyone who came into his aura. People would come to him full of fear and worry. Their fears and worry would drop away and their way would be made dear to them.

The love of God through Yogacharya seemed to be able to overcome all obstacles that devotees brought to him, be it health and healing, as in my case, or business worries, as in the case of many. He could always make it clear to them where they made their mistakes and how to right it. They would all go away inspired, exalted, renewed. He once told me that whenever you meet anyone with whom you have any disharmony, there's something wrong in you. That is a germ that kept me working for years and still does. Pure, divine love alone is the only way we can bridge the gulf.

Annalee Skarin states that if we learn to live the first great commandment of love, we will no longer be under the law, for we will have fulfilled all the laws and prophets and that we will be in contact with God. Each one she says "will be instructed in his actions and the unfolding and perfection of his own life and often foresees God's perfect plan for others. It is a great and holy calling." When I read the above statement in *The Book of Books*, I understood how Yogacharya could understand and instruct all of us in the ways of life in such miraculous fashion. Ways so sublime that none of us who came in contact with him will ever forget.

Christ's words, "Be ye perfect" were immortal and Yogacharya kept us all working at being a saint — if not today, or this incarnation, then tomorrow or as many incarnations as it would take for us to overcome our many layers of negations and to learn to love God and our neighbors.

Annalee Skarin in her works of the further teachings of Christ also states, "to be born of the Spirit is when the pure perfection is fulfilled and one receives a fullness of joy, and only then is his life completely sanctified, and he is given the full power of service in the hands of God." Yogacharya had that joy. He would say, "Nothing can take away my bubble of joy," and he would point toward his heart.

In his book *Loving God,* Chuck Colson begins by saying that the abundance of the Western lifestyle keeps people from developing their soul.

Anna Skarin also tells in her *Book of Books* that the further teaching of Christ is not a devil doctrine of waiting for Christ to come and then exult them into glory. She states we have to purify ourselves first and that here are many who make no effort to overcome the darkness.

Yogacharya was a teacher of the future. He taught people to overcome their bad habits — that was the gist of his life and teachings. People would come to Song of the Morning Ranch for a few years and while they were there he trained them to learn a new way of living, to turn away from their bad habits and replace them with love and light. This training gave people ever-greater joy and ever-greater success, and helped them to find their heart's desire, ever-greater love and light.

For me, he began on my temper, on my resentment and always on my ego and pride. I had a belief in obedience like a dog. He even compared me to a dog at one time. He was pleased with my dogged faith. He could do so much more with people who loved him and worked at overcoming. I was such a person. He only taught according to one's own understanding. He knew that I knew he was working on my "karma." He would show me in an inner conviction just what the outcome would be in each hardship he put me through. I would feel his underlying love and his fabulous consciousness within my consciousness, making me able to overcome one thing after another.

Once, he must have thought I'd gone through enough for that period, for he sent me away. In a miraculous fashion, a friend in Chicago immediately asked me to stay with her and her husband for a couple of weeks. She was shocked (not understanding) the experiences I had gone through. The very next day she came down in the morning and told me how she had seen the incarnations Yogacharya had put me through. She and I both were thrilled with her illuminating visions. Many years later when she lay dying of cancer of the tongue and could not talk she indicated to me that she was having some great vision and she pointed upward. I kept saying questioningly, "You see Yogacharya?" She was so very happy and overjoyed with whomever she saw, and whatever message was given to her, that I too felt happy for her. I never did know who or what she saw, but I felt her inspiration. She died the next day with her family around her.

Another friend who I met at the retreat was a lesbian. Yogacharya treated her with such love and kindness that he drew her from her sordid kind of life which had her so very depressed. Basking in his love like the rest of us, and loving him in her fabulous love and dedication to him, she grew like a weed in beauty of soul. She was an inspiration to me every time I saw her and heard of all the things he would put her through. She understood completely and came through traveling ever upward. Now she was a gal who believed much about astrology and the stars and their parallel in telling of our lives. She felt that she was learning in the stars of a personal disaster to do with water. Yogacharya had warned her to stay away from water. On one particular day she was standing in a bathing suit at the edge of the lake at the ranch where the water was deepest. Yogacharya came along and he jokingly said, "I'm going to push you in the water, Kate." We all laughed, for he often kidded with her. As she also giggled, he repeated his statement, "I'm going to push you in." To the great surprise of the onlookers Yogacharya came up behind her and, unhesitatingly, did push her in the water. She was so shocked, as were all of us standing around, for she could not swim. Through greatly shaken and scared, as we helped her out of the water, she quickly smiled and accepted what he had done. Later she told me how the stars revealed she was to die by drowning. She truly felt that Yogacharya saved her by burning that karma and thus she would not die by drowning. He had saved her life. If I had not seen this experience myself and heard her understanding of it, I might not have believed it. To this day, many, many years later, she lives within the bonding relationship she still has with Yogacharya whom she states is her guru and is leading her through the way of overcoming. His was a path for the strong, and the strong became ever stronger, as does Kate in her ever greater love and work at overcoming the ills in her life.

She was the source of many lesbians coming to Yogacharya, for unlike the so-called Christian, this teacher of an entirely "new age" drew all of them by his great divine love, never, ever condemning a single one. He exemplified God's divine love in everything he did, and everyone was the same to him — we all are imperfect with our many bad habits received so deeply through many incarnations of wrong thinking and living. Yogacharya would often kiddingly say to one or another, "you're worth saving." And so all those who wanted to be saved found their way to the feet of this great saint. He helped all without condemnation or judgment. Some stayed and worked at his retreat and got specialized direction, and others moved and lived close by. Others came every week, every month, and even some once a year. He always knew exactly what they needed, and exactly what their weaknesses were, and always he would amaze everyone who came with his great understanding of them — he was like a mirror and he saw right through their life. It is my hope that people like Kate will be one of the many who will tell of their experiences with Yogacharya and that they can be recorded for all to read — telling the scope of this great teacher who lived amongst us.

Chapter 9 – Unforgettable Love

I'M WRITING THIS to tell of how Annalee Skarin lived and wrote of the further teachings of Christ. Christ said, "The things I do, if you believe, you also can do, and greater things than these also shall you do." This is a statement ignored by most Christians. He further stated that people weren't ready for these further teachings at that time. As one minister has expressed it, the aim is to live in God's glory. Another states Jesus is God. But Jesus stated that we are all sons of God. We too, like Jesus, are created by God. The goal is to be centered in Him. The difference being that Jesus has overcome the world, which we need to do. He admonished "Be ye therefore perfect." He believed we too can overcome the world. It is possible to live the teachings of Christ, not only to read of them and believe.

Annalee Skarin not only wrote of these further teachings. She lived them and showed by her example that they can be lived. Then she went on to say what one will experience if they succeed in doing this. Yogacharya Oliver said there are others who have overcome the world to a very great extent. They have succeeded in peeling off the layers of darkness through many incarnations and are able to reveal the God-self shining through. Annalee Skarin not only overcame the world, but she overcame the last thing to be overcome, death. She succeeded in purifying herself to the degree that she took her body with her. She ascended like Enoch of old. She says we all can do this. It is possible. The time has come. These further teachings must be told about. We too can overcome death and ascend as well.

Having experienced some of the mystery of Yogacharya and having talked to devotees of Paramahansa Yogananda, and also having heard from devotees of Sai Baba, who lives today in India, leads me to believe that there are very likely countless others. I'm convinced there are hundreds of others. Maurice Burke in his book entitled *Cosmic Consciousness* said it would be so for this century. Years ago Burke wrote that more and more highly developed spiritual souls would he born into our world.

The Bible says, "Without faith, it is impossible to please God." Faith is the dream, the desire, and is hope itself. And by faith it can be established in the realm of tangible substance and become forever the reality.

Annalee Skarin says men are "Gods in the making," and when and if we live the teachings, we will know it. She says we must pray without ceasing and repent and do good works, and unto such will he revealed that which has never been revealed. This centuries-old promise still stands.

She further states that her last book, *The Book of Books,* is for the pure of heart, the humble, the teachable, the gracious, the evolving sons of God. Not for those who are sealed in their present beliefs, but for those who are hungering and thirsting after righteousness — the straight and narrow path that leads to Life Eternal.

She states it is the Pathway of Love in which one practices and learns to love God with all his heart and thus he will be cleansed of all sin. The very forgiveness of sin can only be accomplished through love that can forgive all that has transpired against him. This is love in action: the love that can cleanse. She says this pathway is a Holy Trail, God-lighted, of ever increasing brilliance. Her book helped me to understand the glowing faces of Yogacharya and Daya Mata, and many others who reach a glowing state from time to time.

Yogacharya was such a great example that this great divine love does exist and can be reached by steadfast patience and practice. Just as a piano player must practice and practice to reach perfection, so must we practice sending out love to reach these higher states of forgiving, of love divine. The one who loves greatly radiates it, as did Yogacharya.

Annalee Skarin states that the door to this glorious Path of joy and gladness and increasing enlightenment and understanding is contained fully in the divine First Great Commandment of all power: Love!

Live the laws and you will know — so said Christ. And none can possibly know anything unless he experiences it. To hear about things and conditions of God may be part of one's beliefs but never becomes a part of his actual knowledge until he experiences it for himself. Live the first and great commandment and the second will follow naturally. You won't need any other teacher but God himself. One's every cell, fiber, and atom of one's being must become imbued with that living love.

Annalee Skarin says that the developing and releasing of love from the heart, soul, and mind overcomes all negation, dislikes, fears, unhappiness, weakness, ugliness, and mortal grubbiness. These traits will be dissolved. Such a one will automatically become that Love. Live the laws admonished by Christ "And you will know." Man has never accepted the dynamic challenge to LIVE Christ's teaching. She further writes in her book, "Man has only weakly affirmed his inactive endorsement of these teachings as a fullness of acceptance. And many think they are proving their belief by going forth and hammering others with their interpretations as they send forth their haranguements in discordant, sanctimonious self-righteousness. Christ's actual teachings have never been acknowledged as a way of life and fulfillment."

The first and great commandment when lived contains the breathtaking fulfillment of every Promise that God gave. Within it is held the fulfilling of love — the LOVE which brings to one's life a complete knowledge of the things which "Eye has never seen nor ears heard, neither hath entered into the heart of man those unspeakable glories which God has PREPARED FOR THOSE WHO LOVE HIM" — and prove day to day their living of that law pertaining to it. This commandment must be LIVED. This requires an extended effort of constant desire and appreciation until the very cells of the body and brain and heart sing together in a glory of joyous response at the slightest suggestion or thought of God, or of His blessings. It is as that LOVE is developed that it will finally take over in every cell and fiber and thus that one "transforms his carnal flesh, to flesh divine without descending through the gates of death — even as Enoch of old accomplished. Truly born of the Spirit and the shame of his mortal nakedness, (whatever the cause) it will be overcome and he will "comprehend all things."

Annalee Skarin further states "And this is God's Plan. And it has always been His plan. And this is the Way Christ traveled. It is the path He mapped out for all mankind to follow: TO OVERCOME."

Yogacharya did not reach a state of ascending and taking his body with him. At the end of the book there is an account of his death written by Peggy Braden who was with him when he made his transition. An account of the passing of Paramahansa Yogananda is written by SRF, as he too left his body as planned.

Bob Raymer, the present spiritual leader at Yogacharya's Song of the Morning Retreat has told me that he has proof of the ascension of Annalee Skarin and since I am able to believe that death can be overcome, I completely accept what Mr. Raymer has said. There are also many fantastic stories and accounts of the state of divine love to which Yogacharya reached, as told by many devotees who knew him.

A Sudden Goodbye

When I lost my mother in 1968, I had taken her on a trip to Ireland. Though she was 84, I felt she would "be all right," because I had asked Yogacharya before we went. I always believed everything he told me, so I felt secure, even though she had a bad heart. Well, his idea of "all right" was apparently different from mine, for she died on the first day of the tour.

I was very close to my mother and loved her dearly. Looking back I consoled myself, much later, that she really did have as good a death as one could have. We were going to a banquet on the tour, and we were waiting in the hotel lobby for the bus to arrive. I couldn't help noticing that my mother never looked prettier than she did that evening. I had gone to the window, saw the bus in the distance, and came back to the side of my mother to notify her. As I came close, I noticed a strange look on her face and in alarm I exclaimed, "Mother, are you all right?" She had been sitting with her back away from the chair, and as I spoke and reached her, it was as if she was waiting for me to be there before she left her body. It was at that moment that she leaned back in the chair, and she was gone. I called frantically and looked at her eyes which already were dilated fully. I knew it was the end. I walked away and sat on a close-by chair in a state of shock. It was as if there were a screen between the people surrounding my mother trying to revive her and myself. Apparently, everything was "all right," for while her body was still in the chair, a couple came over to me and announced they were from Chicago (where we were living at the time). Completely strangers, but, nevertheless, they took over and called my relatives in Nova Scotia, the undertaker, and whatever else had to be done. They stayed with me all evening and until the next day when they were leaving. I was content to go wherever they took me. They made arrangements for a sister I had in England to come there. They took me to meet her at the airport when they left for Chicago. My sister was with me for a day and then an Archbishop of the Church of England appeared on the scene and stayed with me until I was taken to the airport by him. At no time was I left alone for those three days when I had to stay in Ireland. When my mother's body and I arrived in Halifax, Nova Scotia, my family and I went through the funeral, and I quickly returned to Chicago. The day I arrived back in Chicago, an acquaintance called to say he was going to Yogacharya's retreat. This was just one more of those miraculous events that took place, for the young man who called did not know that I had lost my mother, nor was he a friend who would be calling ordinarily.

We went to the retreat, but I was still in such a deep state of depression and shock that I just sat in one place. I sat where I knew Yogacharya would soon arrive. I was so very eager to see him, but at the same time vexed with him for telling me that my mother would be "all right."

As I scanned the entrance at the bottom of the hill, Yogacharya's car came in and then went out. It came in and went out, again. I could stand it no longer. So I got up, and with another young man, (for the place was filled with young devotees), I decided I would go raspberry picking far into the woods — a long way from where Yogacharya would be "coming in and going out." I wanted to get as far away as possible, I thought to myself, for I was convinced he did not care of the pain I felt.

When the young man and I arrived at a far distance from the ranch, (for the grounds has 800 acres of property surrounding the retreat) we were busy picking raspberries when we heard a car. Now the property has lots of little paths but none that could hold a car, as far as I knew. It seemed a tremendous miracle to us to see a car there. The young man exclaimed, "Look! It's Yogacharya!"

"It can't be," I said, looking in the distance as the car drove by. "He doesn't have a hat like that."

When we returned to the retreat, Yogacharya was standing there, surrounded by devotees. Lo and behold, he did have on that hat. He had actually taken a trip into those woods with a Cadillac car. I suddenly knew he had come there to let me know he did care, of that I was certain. I considered that fantastic love and a fantastic way of telling me he cared.

Later we had dinner at the caretaker's place. Yogacharya had me sit beside him and, as he said grace, I burst into tears, the first since the death of my mother. Yogacharya had helped me to open my heart. Once again I saw he had such magical ways of helping people in need.

While I had been sitting on the hillside watching his car come in and out earlier, I had been thinking in my frustration to see him: "Wouldn't it be wonderful to have a chance just to walk with him holding my hand, much as a young monk once told me of Paramahansa Yogananda doing with him — just walking and not saying anything — just the closeness that was so healing, from a spiritual giant like Yogananda (for him), and from Yogacharya (for me) — that divine healing love that could set everything straight?

Well, we had finished our dinner, and Yogacharya was still surrounded by devotees, all as eager as I to be close to him, so I went outside, feeling it was impossible to get near him. I wasn't there half a minute when, again, miraculously, he was beside me, taking my hand in his and leading me down the road in silence.

That was divine love in action, a love you could never forget.

Chapter 10 – Working Wonders with Everyone

ANNALEE SKARIN STATES in her *Book of Books* how man may practice Christ's further teaching. She states we have to do this on God's terms. She states Faith is composed of the highest vibrations released from a human heart. And she says Faith in action is belief held forth on a high level of anticipation as doubts are banished. Faith is power — it is super-energized thought and feeling and can build highways to the stars. She states that without Faith, it is impossible to please God. She says it is perfected by use. Christ says, "Knock and it will be opened, seek and you will find, know the Truth and the Truth will make you free." Annalee Skarin states this life is a school for Gods, though not all will attain that perfection. Each selects his goal and reaches it according to his desire. Devils destroy but God's own are creators.

Christ said live the teachings and you will know God's promise is bringing forth good works. Pray without ceasing, and it will be given unto such to know the mysteries of God. "Yea, unto such it shall be given to reveal things which never have been revealed; yes, it shall be given unto such to bring thousands of souls to repentance." Though this promise was given centuries ago, it still stands today.

Yogacharya reached a very high state of spiritual development and, my having read Annalee Skarin's *Book of Books*, it has given me a much greater understanding of Yogacharya as a messenger of God. He was truly an advanced spiritual man of God with seemingly no ego. He cared not what people thought of him, He said exactly what people needed to hear, regardless of their reactions, or reactions of those around him. If it was something a soul needed to hear in order to go up to the next step of the spiritual ladder, he'd say or do what was necessary. He was a true channel of God. Selfless to the very end — he did not build an organization. When he left this world, he left behind a retreat, which nearly fell apart at his departure. But before that could happen, a divine soul whom Yogacharya had known years earlier would come there and take charge, and today his retreat flourishes.

I have heard it said that Sai Baba of India is God incarnate — for he does such fabulous miracles. Perhaps so. I never met or experienced his miracles. I heard though, that he has brought people back to life, and has even produced life itself, along with other fabulous experiences. Lots of people came to Yogacharya's retreat with tales of Sai Baba and movies of all kinds. Still, of great spiritual leaders who were known for great things, Yogacharya would regard all of them as elementary. When people brought him tales and movies of Sai Baba, he said nothing but would watch the movies over and over again. Sai Baba amongst his thousands of devotees who clamored for his attention was impressive. Sai Baba would send Americans to Yogacharya and would tell some of them that Yogacharya was their guru — being someone who knows God and can teach others how to find God. A devotee who had returned from India recently told me that Sai Baba stated that Yogacharya was the greatest master on the American continent. I replied that I had always thought that, and the devotee said that that statement from Sal Baba was very recent.

The reason I thought he was the greatest master was because of his lack of ego. As I saw it, he seemed to live his life entirely to teach others how to live their lives successfully, showing all the errors they were making and what steps to take next for the sake of their spiritual development. He seemed to know each and every person who came before him intimately — their weaknesses and their strengths. They, in turn, would recognize in him his great wisdom, his divine love, his magnetism, and his ability to see through just about every experience life brought to the people whom the Lord sent to him.

I remember a woman who had a grave problem with her partner in business. He told her exactly what to do to save her business from a great loss. When a couple came to him and were about to divorce, he showed them just how to divide up their possessions to the satisfaction of both of them. When a Jewish man came to him and talked about his religion, he soon found out that Yogacharya knew much more about his Jewish religion than he did.

With the young people who came to him he would often put them in jobs that would cause them to open up and bloom like a flower. Others, he had working together, and then he was able to instill his consciousness into them at times, when necessary, to show them how to react to situations where they failed. He would then remove his consciousness and lead them to a similar experience for them to try again. If they failed again, the situation would keep coming up, until they mastered it. The mastering of each fault or difficulty would then lead to an even greater difficulty or obstacle to face. Thus, the devotee would work at ever-greater improvements of all of his weaknesses and faults. People who once would meet Yogacharya would have their faults and weaknesses mirrored back at them. Until that time, they would go along — as it always is with people who thought like they did — in a "comfort zone" free of worries. Only those who had a desire to be better and do better did he take under his tutelage. Others would seem wander off and he would help to usher them on their way. But for those who were tuned into his love and magnetism, he brought miraculous changes into their lives.

I remember one woman whom he taught great practices for dealing with children. She had brought up two children in the past, and likely he knew that in the future she would bring up her grandson. For even after Yogacharya was gone from this earth, she could recall the many experiences she had with children while he was here and could continue to apply her many lessons to her latest challenge. He made everything a tremendous challenge every day, as new and greater faults would come up. Apparently, we all have a vast storage place of faults and experiences to be relived and brought to consciousness in order to overcome them and progress to a higher stage of understanding and spiritual knowledge.

Jealousy was a great fault that lots of people had. He would play one against the other so as to bring it out. Once in the open, a devotee would work very hard to overcome it. There seemed no end to the depths of some people who suffered from jealousy. He never tired of letting people live experience after experience in order to rid themselves of jealousy.

Bad temper was another. He would create situations to bring out one's bad temper. After many experiences, one would finally get control. Getting control of everything seemed to be a goal, along with learning ever-greater love. Love will completely erase everything negative. We all seemed to have a great storage place of hatreds, fears, jealousies, and lacks of all kinds. He knew everyone who came to him, just what that person had to work on, what he had to overcome, and he would tirelessly give everyone his love and his great consciousness to help in whatever was the devotee's endeavor.

One day a woman came to dinner. He must have known she had a great desire to marry. There were about twelve people at the table, and during the conversation he went on a great tirade about people wanting to marry and how they lived life like a slob, left everything around, never cleaned up after themselves, etc. This woman who hardly knew him knew he was talking to her. After the meal, she became so irritated that she nearly left then and there. But his loving and sweet ways following his "tirade" made her soon forget her anger. She later told me the story and how she went home and started clearing away the table and making so many changes in her lifestyle that one day her younger brother asked, "What happened to you at that yoga camp?"

Yogacharya always knew how to approach everyone —
what they could take and what they were unable to take.
My dear mother was very shy where Yogacharya was
concerned. At one glance he knew that she was a great
soul and so he treated her with such great tenderness,
kindness, and love that, even though she was in her
seventies when she met him, he inspired a great desire in
her to improve, just as he did in younger people.

One young man had so many problems that he
suffered from a great stomach disorder. On his first visit
to Yogacharya he was in a class with about 40 or 50
people, but he came out of the class with tremendous
enthusiasm, because he was sure Yogacharya was
speaking directly to him. Yogacharya was able to give
many people at the same time answers to many
problems and experiences. He knew their lives
intimately and knew their complete situations. As one
woman said to me one day, "That is exactly how it is in
my office." He always knew exactly how it was in the
office and life of everyone who crossed his path. He
truly seemed to have all the powers of God in his great
knowledge of the lives of everyone, all at the same time.

When he heard someone talk of the miracles of
Sai Baba, I couldn't help thinking of the great miracles
of Yogacharya as he revealed his great knowledge of the
lives of everyone that even came near him. His
knowledge of people and their lives, their weaknesses
and strengths, was mind-boggling to me. It was no
wonder that at the time I first met him, as I mentioned in
the first chapter, when I sat at a table of about 16 or 17,
he being seated in the middle, I thought to myself who
was this man? Was he God? Or What? As he talked to

everyone at the other end of the table suddenly I was brought out of my reverie. He turned his head in my direction and his eyes fell on me as he said, (this was in the midst of his conversation with the other people), "Well, I'll tell you one thing. God isn't a man!" There was no doubt in my mind hut that he was answering my thoughts. From that day forth, I found this sort of thing happening all the time, every time I was in his company. I had to mend my thoughts, for he always knew them!

When I told this to my mother, she wouldn't believe me at first. But when she met him he treated her with such kindness, love, and respect that, from that moment on, she became like a teenager, like the rest of us.

Well, I'll tell you one thing, when Yogacharya said, "God isn't a man," that sentence gave me much trouble, for I knew he knew my thoughts. The Evangelicals say Jesus is God, but having had the experience of spending much time with Yogacharya, I no longer doubt but believe strongly that Yogacharya had great love and respect for Jesus. His own father had had an encounter with Jesus, he once told us, but he said his father could go no farther on the spiritual path because of his sealed mind at his present level. Yogacharya said we must have open minds.

Chapter 11 – In the Hearts of All

ANNALEE SKARIN STATES in her *Book of Books*, "Only love can possibly purify the heart."

Everything Yogacharya did came from a pure heart of love.

I talked to a friend on the phone a week ago and I said, "Tell me one experience (and she has had thousands) that I can put in my book before I finish it."

She was a homosexual and she had had a tough life of persecution. When she first came, she was "brow-beaten" and forlorn. Yogacharya knew "exactly" her whole life — like he did everyone, who came his way. He gave her so much love and kindness it was beautiful to see — divine love, as only he knew how to give it, and he gave it from the earliest days he met her. I remember one cute little incident that I witnessed, and that she told me about, at the time. She told me that before coming to the service that Sunday morning, she had taken a shower and when, she came out of the shower room, she waved a kiss to Yogacharya's picture sitting on her bureau in her bedroom. After coming to the service and attempting to come close to Yogacharya in the fellowship room where everyone was crowding around him, she noticed standing room only, on all sides. So she waved to him over the heads of the crowd with the intention of leaving. He waved back and blew her a kiss. Needless to say, she was more thrilled than the crowd who pressed so close, for she knew

Yogacharya had received her wave and kiss from earlier in the morning.

One day, years later, she remembers she was feeling very sad, having been told by her friend that Yogacharya had given her (the friend) a big bear hug; she replied sadly to the friend that he had never given her a big hug. Later that same day, she was climbing the stairs leading to the lodge at Yogacharya's retreat when she noticed some feet at the top. She looked up and there was Yogacharya with his arms open wide. She was thrilled again as he gave her a big bear hug.

After Yogacharya left us in 1989, once again she was very sad. It was her habit to become acquainted with all the Eastern Swamis that came from India. She loved all the Indian Saints that would arrive in Detroit from time to time. Then one day there was one from a monastic order that apparently did not talk very much or was very demonstrative. But when he saw her he said, "I see you are missing your guru very much." And then to her surprise he gave her a big hug and she heard Yogacharya's voice saying in her ear, "I'm giving you a hug through Swami." She told me on the phone that she feels his presence leading her every day since he left.

Everyone had a unique bond with Yogacharya known only to the devotee and Yogacharya, and this gal had a very unique bond, indeed, and always did have, for the thirty years that I have known her.

Her great love for Yogacharya drove her away from the homosexual way of life and today she tells me she doesn't go many places anymore because she feels the Presence so much, she doesn't like to be separated from it. She brought many of her homosexual friends in the earlier days to see Yogacharya. Those who wished to lead a better life he gave of his great divine love. As Annalee Skarin said, "It is only divine love that can purify the heart."

Years ago there was a girl who would sit on the floor and take notes on everything Yogacharya would say. She had always been curious as to what her name means, and, without her asking, one day he said her name meant "joy." And she was joyous, all the time.

One night he came to her in a dream and she told me there was a time in the dream for fun at first, and then he told her "destruction at night." She had a sickly mother in a nursing home and so she thought she was about to lose her mother, but it was her 18 year old daughter who suddenly died the next evening

Before Yogacharya started the retreat and moved there permanently, several devotees and my mother and I visited the Ranch. When they all left and Yogacharya went back to Detroit, my mother and I stayed on for the following week, alone. You might say we acted as caretakers. We stripped the beds, except for the one room where Yogacharya stayed. His bed had not been slept in. When he returned at the end of the week, I asked him, "You didn't sleep in that bed last weekend?" He replied, "Was there a bed there?" I guess I assumed he meditated all night.

Another day when his daughter was having a great coughing spell during meditation, I happened to have opened my eyes just as I saw him reach out and touch her. The coughing stopped for the rest of the meditation, His every wish seemed to be fulfilled, or so it seemed.

When my half-brother died in California many years ago, I joined my sister there. We did not know what to do, so I meditated that morning. Despite my anxiety, I had a great meditation and felt a real Presence. Afterwards we went to the SRF Mother Center in Los Angeles and received the name of a lawyer from a devotee there. We turned everything over to him and were glad to get out from under all the difficulties of the paperwork. When we returned to the motel and told acquaintances what we had done, one man asked us, "Was he a probate lawyer?" When he heard that he was not, he ridiculed us. However, I know that feeling of the Presence could not be denied. I replied, "All will be Okay, I have faith!" To make a long story short, it turned out that the law had been changed that very day. This enabled me, the only sister living in the states (since I lived in Illinois), to name this lawyer as the executor of the estate. My other three sisters lived in Halifax, Nova Scotia, and his real sister lived in Australia.

My sister and I were then able to return home. I returned to Chicago and she to Halifax. The lawyer, despite not being a probate lawyer, knew that the law had been changed that very day. He sent copies of everything he did to my three sisters in Nova Scotia, to me in Chicago, and to the one sister in Australia. In five months, he finished the entire probate procedure and only charged us 3%. The English Embassy in Australia had advised my sister living there (she was born in England, along with the brother who died) to get her own lawyer. He said the lawyer would request 5%. It seemed like another miracle to me! I gave 10% of the inheritance that I received to the retreat and I felt very blessed.

There was a great saint in India called Anandamoyee Ma. When one of Yogacharya's devotees from Detroit went touring in India "seeking her guru," she wound up at the feet of Anandamoyee Ma. She asked Ma, "Who is my guru?" The woman Saint replied, "When the devotee is willing to go to the ends of the earth to find her guru [teacher], she will find him in her own back yard!" So she returned, and I was present when she told Yogacharya of Anandamoyee Ma's answer.

Yogacharya still comes to people in dreams. A young man who had once been the manager of the retreat had a dream visit by Yogacharya in which he told him to leave and return to school. He told me about it himself and that he always wanted to do that, so, despite the protests of the spiritual leader at the retreat, he did leave and returned to school.

One day quite recently, I saw a woman devotee that I hadn't seen since Yogacharya left and I exclaimed, "You haven't been here since 1989 when you came for Yogacharya's memorial service, how did you happen to come here today?" She replied that Yogacharya came to her in a dream and told her to come.

He has been known to appear to people in the flesh as well. One young man, (now a lawyer but at that time a hippie) traveled to the Caribbean dock to do some thinking. Suddenly, there was Yogacharya standing on the sand on the beach where he was. He got such a shock, he jumped back into his car and returned to the retreat. It was the time of the "hippies" and he lived that lifestyle back then. He came back, changed to a normal lifestyle, settled down, and lived at the retreat for a while. Then he got involved in a romance with a girl on the staff. Yogacharya sent them both away. He would not have romance at the retreat. He said, "The paths at the retreat were not going to be lovers' lanes." Then they came back and were married at the retreat by Yogacharya.

An old friend told me of some experiences he had with Yogacharya. He said he wanted to go jogging but the pull to meditate was so great that he gave up the jogging idea and sat at the feet of Yogacharya's picture to meditate. As he gazed at the picture, he said it slowly changed and became real — as if Yogacharya were alive — and he could even ask him questions. From that day forth, he learned that he could bring him back whenever he really wanted to see him — thus, Yogacharya kept him ever on the path of seeking God further and further within.

In earlier years, this same friend wanted to join the staff of the ranch. Yogacharya appeared to him dressed as a carpenter. He then enrolled in a course in carpentry and later he was accepted on the staff.

Chapter 12 – The Power to Change Lives

CHRIST SAID there was much more he had to teach but that the world is not ready yet. It would seem to those of us who knew Yogacharya Oliver that he was one of those "chosen ones," for there is no doubt that he reached a high level of consciousness and oneness with God. There is no doubt in my mind but that there is a new era being ushered in — one of light and love. Thousands of us are witnesses to the fact that this life of the further teachings of Christ was lived by Yogacharya Oliver. The miracles he did every day became commonplace to those who knew him. They were so subtle that all but a relatively few became aware at the time, but now that he is gone, many more are becoming aware. I will tell of many of these experiences to show the world that indeed it is a new age.

Only those blessed by God's light and love will become aware, but there will be lots of people who will recognize the truth. Yogacharya had learned to harness his mind and control his thoughts and to push his ego aside. He thus lived a completely selfless life for God.

Annalee Skarin says the power in love is greater than the power of hate, and in this new age upcoming we will learn to rule ourselves and then, by the power of God, we will go forth in power and love and become sons and daughters of God. She says to do this we must live each moment as we desire the future to be. She says the power of God is as great today as in the days of Christ and is waiting to be brought forth in the heart of any man who is prepared to receive it. Now is the time for those who are ready to evolve.

Man must recognize and love the indwelling Christ in his own being and then he will recognize the Christ-self in others. They will recognize their true inner being by loving the Christ within. All faults and weaknesses can be overcome by the Christ within.

Yogacharya had such a love — a love that could allow everyone to be free. He would listen to everyone, and seemingly God spoke to him through everyone. He was such a great example in every way. He always stated that humility was the key to power.

Annalee Skarin says that each man is the designer of his own calamities and his own downfall, as well as the creator of his own glories. Romans 8:14-17 states: "For as many as are led by the Spirit of God, they are the sons of God. And, if children, then heirs; heirs of God, and joint heirs of Christ."

In Philippians 2:5-6 it states, "Let this mind be in you which was also in Christ Jesus,…Who, being in the form of God thought it not robbery to be equal with God." In Revelation 12:6-7 it states: "He that overcometh shall inherit all things and I will be his God and he shall be my son."

And so we shall see how this fabulous man, Yogacharya Oliver, fit into these sayings of the Bible. He taught people to be real — not to act as their ego made them feel but to learn to love and act out of love instead of ego. The biggest thing he taught me was to learn to rely on the Presence within (call it God, Christ-consciousness, inner being — we all feel an inner Presence) and allow that Presence to love through me, just as I felt Yogacharya did for me those years I was with him as my "teacher" (or guru).

To experience this purity and love, one must clean the outside of the cup (way of thinking, way of feeling, of being). Annalee Skarin says, "To him who will only see the inner purification of love, nothing is impossible to him."

All truly great works are done from this "power within," not human intellect. And most truly spiritual people do try to live in this divine inner light — the joy of a Christ-conscious state. And as Christ said, "Come unto me, all who are heavy-laden," and he would give rest, so also Yogacharya had that ability to give rest to the heavy-laden. Those were the kind of seekers who found their way to him.

Yogacharya taught everyone to learn to meditate and listen to that inner voice. The Bible says, "Be still and know that I am God." That is the big thing we must all learn. We can all hear that inner voice, the Voice of God, if we will take the time to slow down and get quiet regularly.

Someone once asked Yogacharya, "How do you know when you hear the inner voice?"

He replied, "There is a bubble of joy that accompanies the answer."

I have a friend who has been going to the retreat almost as long as I have. He recently told me that when he first began to come to the temple in Detroit where

Yogacharya held services at the Art Institute in the 60's, he disliked everyone and everything. I remember him coming to the services and how cynical he was and how he'd make hurtful remarks to people and laughed out loud at their simple beliefs — a real "smart aleck" attitude! Then one day as he sat in the first row below the platform where Yogacharya sat to conduct his Sunday service, this friend suddenly became filled with a great love — a divine love. The tears came running down his cheeks, so much so, he described it, that he couldn't contain it. It was an overwhelming experience given to him by Yogacharya, to show him what it is to love instead of hate, as had been his negative habit.

When I had been given a similar experience, I was amazed when the "great divine love" was taken away, that I had such little love of my own to give to others.

From that time on, both of us, the friend and I, attempted to develop greater love than we were able to experience at the time. Now, 40 years later, when I see my friend at the retreat, we often reminisce as to how Yogacharya changed our lives and inspired us like no other to seek God and to learn to love.

I talked to another old-timer who was at the Ranch when Yogacharya was there and who has managed the Ranch and also did most of the cooking (he even gave seminars on vegetarian cooking). He was working, managing a restaurant in Florida, when Yogacharya left his body. Shortly afterwards Yogacharya came to him in a dream and told him to go to the Ranch and "feed my people." He immediately dropped everything, resigned his job in Florida, and returned to the retreat, spending many more years there, cooking and planning the meals, as well as doing other jobs at the Ranch that needed to be done. He is a conscientious devotee of God alone and has been so all of these years since Yogacharya left the body.

Chapter 13 – The Words of Annalee Skarin and the Manifestation of One of God's Special Sons, Yogacharya Oliver

Know the truth and the truth will make you free

ANNALEE SKARIN SAYS, "This earth is the school for learning how to become Gods, but not all students will fulfill so great an assignment, but that many will. Those who assume the responsibility of living up to their highest inborn instincts will evolve into Godhood. Gods are creators, and men are Gods in the making."

My teacher, Yogacharya Oliver, as we called him, was a living manifestation of much of what Annalee Skarin wrote. In Revelation 21:6-7 it says, "He that overcometh, shall inherit all things; and I will be His God and he shall be my son," This all seemed to be so in my observation of Yogacharya Oliver. Annalee further says, "Man has never accepted the dynamic challenge to live Christ's teachings." She says we must live it and we will know — and no one can possibly know anything unless he himself experiences it.

To hear about things and conditions of God may become part of one's beliefs, but never become part of his actual knowledge until he experiences it for himself. Like stated in the first great commandment — love, and you will know: And you will need none to teach you, for God Himself will be your teacher. To fulfill it requires that every cell, fiber, and atom of one's being be imbued with it. Only then does it become a part of one's experience, part of the living tissues of his heart, mind, and soul, until they not only become a very part of his being, they become him, and he becomes that LOVE. Live the first and great commandment and the second will follow naturally without effort or striving. This developing and releasing of LOVE from the HEART, MIND, and SOUL overcomes all negation, dislikes, fears, ugliness, weaknesses, and all human grubbiness, for these traits will be dissolved — and such a one will become that LOVE.

Christ's actual teachings have never been acknowledged as a Way of Life and fulfillment or an everlasting privilege of stupendous accomplishment, crowned with every reward in every Promise ever given since time began.

And this is God's plan. And it has always been His plan. It is the Path He mapped out for all mankind to follow, if they wished to rise above dreary mortality and its consequent evils, dismays, and vicissitudes.

Our intuition tells us that whether we are Protestant, Catholic, or Yogis, we all agree, love is the way, the one thing common to all religions and philosophies.

Annalee Skarin says, "God's terms are not different when one is sincere and determined and filled with love. And his Promises are offered to every living soul upon earth — every layman, every minister, and every member of every church, and to those without any church affiliation whatsoever. They pertain to all mankind. They have not been fulfilled because self-righteous leaders have assumed that their congregations or followers can only go to God through their mediating, which is the great error. Every living soul has the right and the initiative standing forth to KNOW GOD for themselves. The fruit of the tree of life is the love of God. A love which is shed forth through the hearts of the children of men. And only love can possibly purify the heart."

Annalee Skarin says her book is not written for the unbelievers or for those who love not God — or for those who are so sealed in their present beliefs that God cannot teach them. She says this work (from which I'm quoting) is for the pure in heart, the humble, the teachable, the gracious, evolving sons of God. "It is for those who are hungering and thirsting after righteousness!' And she says every step of the way is a joy beyond measure. The very forgiveness of sin can be accomplished. This is love in action! Let hurts be dissolved in compassionate understanding. You will join the gods in the upward trend of your own divinity. So the nearer man approaches perfection, the clearer are his views and the greater their enjoyments.

All of us who spent time around Yogacharya Oliver knew this to be true. He always had his bubble of joy, and I marvel again and again that there seemed little that he didn't know about anyone. Whenever any devotee came before him, he seemed to know them well — even those who weren't devotees — he would know them so well. He would know everyone's strong points and weak, their drives and interests and goals in life. He seemed to know it all.

Chapter 14 – God Alone

IN THE VERY EARLY YEARS, shortly after meeting Yogacharya and after being convinced that he was my guru, I was very torn by the teachings about gurus given by Paramahansa Yogananda wherein he said he was the last of the line of Self-Realization gurus. The line being Babaji, Lahiri Mahasaya, Sri Yukteswar, and Paramahansa Yogananda. I felt without a doubt that Yogananda was not my guru. How did it all fit?

One day while meditating in front of the pictures of these gurus, Babaji, Lahiri Mahasaya, Sri Yukteswar, and Yogananda, I became very disturbed, because I believed in, *both* Yogananda, *and* Yogacharya. I just could not find peace of mind! There was a terrible inner conflict. Suddenly, the fact that Yogacharya was actually an incarnation of Lahiri Mahasaya sprang up in my mind, like a light going on. I immediately felt tremendous peace and joy, having found the answer to my conflict. And I was able to meditate after that. Because I was new to the Self-Realization teachings and organizations, I accepted this without question for many years. That was before I realized that Yogacharya and Lahiri Mahasaya had both been in the world for a few hours at the same time.

It was many years later that I happened to visit a Swami Bhashyananda of the Vedanta Society of Chicago and was able to ask him about this. The Vedanta Temple was only a few blocks from where I lived in Chicago (most of my life) and I knew Swami Bhashyananda, having visited the Temple on occasion and met him several times. If was Swami's habit to come to his sitting room on the first floor every afternoon, and he would receive people there. I knew a young devotee who was staying at the Vedanta Temple, so I made arrangements through him to come and see Swami one afternoon. It was as though he were expecting me to ask my question, for he answered almost before I told my story. He said, "Oh, yes, it was quite possible for the same soul to be in Yogacharya and Lahiri Mahasaya for that short period of time."

We then went on to have a great chat for nearly an hour before I left. After I left his company, the young devotee I knew who lived there told me I shouldn't be tiring Swami, that he had had a stroke and no longer was able to receive visitors in the sitting room and especially not have conversations with them. He said Swami always slurs his words and can't talk plainly. Imagine my surprise, because, for my entire interview, he showed no signs of a stroke nor of slurring his words nor even of being tired. On the contrary, he seemed to be expecting me and was eager to talk and was very animated. I felt very blessed and at peace after my visit with him. And I felt what he had to say confirmed my inmost feelings about the truth of the relationship between Yogacharya and Lahiri Mahasaya.

My life with Yogacharya was full of ups and downs and contained much anguish. He knew I had great will power from the beginning and that I would work at overcoming great challenges. So it turned out that, after he won my love, he provided many challenges and obstacles. He noticed I was always eager to tackle anything and everything. One day, when someone felt sorry for me and asked him why he treated me as he did, he simply replied, "Betty needs to be treated like that." When I heard about it, I just laughed, for I knew he was right in his treatment. I knew that it inspired me to work harder at climbing the spiritual ladder. Whenever he was very hard on me, he would throw me a crumb, so to speak, with a sudden kindness or bit of praise. And so I was always content with just that much reward. I guess I was an odd one. I always thought it was because my parents were English. Anyway, we understood each other and somehow I always knew what he was teaching me and that it was just "the divine play." I enjoyed all his challenges and when he felt it was too much for me, he would send me away. People looking on couldn't begin to understand what it was all about, but I did, and I knew that he knew me like a book. I got tremendous enjoyment out of the fact that he knew me so very well. He always did and said the exact right thing at the right moment.

Because I had so much drive to go to the next step up the spiritual ladder Yogacharya was like "an extension of the arm of God" to provide me the next step, and the next step. Perhaps that was why he was so often heard to say, "I have no will of my own." He seemed to be a pure channel of God, especially when dealing with devotees who were apparently sent to him by God. There were often many whom he sent to other paths (and I'd often wonder why, when it was apparent they were inspired by him). But as he'd say to me, "Let things happen and don't try to make them happen." He would always do just that. He knew what everyone's next step was, and he'd be that extension of God and direct them on their way.

At the very beginning when I first came to him and he began to poke and prod me to bring out anger, at that time he also showed me how it affected him to be that channel to cause me to come up over the obstacles. He would have tears in his eyes. From this, I felt it meant I must give up my anger. It had to go. I worked on this week after week after week, before I felt I had it under control. Without him giving me the treatment I needed, I would never have come up over it, I don't believe. That was the way he provided obstacles and challenges to me, right from the beginning, and all through my entire time with him. I remember back in those days I happened to see a short movie on TV where British and Americans were going on vacation at this resort. The English were assigned rooms with the strangest, most difficult circumstances while the Americans had an easy time of it. I knew at once that I belonged to that strange breed of people! God must have showed me that movie for a reason!

One time, when he sent me back to Chicago, because he thought, "I couldn't take it anymore," I can't recall how long I stayed there, nor the circumstances as to how I went back to Yogacharya "for more." But I did go back after a few years. Though my life was full of ups and downs around Yogacharya, I loved to be there, for I grew like a weed up the spiritual ladder. He used to say that when you get enough in your spiritual bank account, then you'd see how worthwhile everything was. I guess I must have been trying for the big bank account, for I kept praying for this and that test. The person who had a lukewarm desire to go forward, or none at all, led a quiet life with no, or very, few ups and downs.

Two weeks before he left us, he sent me away again. This time I was really devastated, for I didn't understand it this time. I had come up over the obvious things and I had no idea what was wrong. He had taught me to write letters when I was devastated, so I was writing and writing, when someone called and told me that Yogacharya had left his body. I felt his loving presence once more, but never after that. That is, it was not like I used to feel it. He was always saying to me that he would not have people being dependent on him. I

Betty and Yogacharya, 1975.

never knew what he meant and why he'd always say that to me, for he was always surrounded by people who were completely dependent on him while I lived in Chicago for the most part of our relationship. He said, too, that the disciple was like a flower standing in the wind, tied to a stick. As the plant got stronger, the stick was taken away. So he said it was like that with the guru and disciple. When the disciple got stronger, the guru wasn't needed.

But he was never very far away. He had told a friend to tell me to go to Chicago (where I would feel isolated) and thus, I soon had a prayer relationship going with God alone. I had been well trained in communicating with a Presence for about thirty years. After I received a card from Peter in which Yogacharya told me I was "in his heart," I then felt content. I felt blessed to have had such a teacher for so many years. And now I realized God alone was to be my teacher. I didn't seem to need a teacher in the flesh anymore. And when I did have a great need, someone or other was always there for me. I didn't try to analyze who, for I knew they were all one — God and all the great masters and saints of all religions. Be it Christian, Buddhist, Hindu, or any other.

As Annie Kirkwood put it in her *Mary's Message to the World*, Mary, Mother of Jesus, comes to her regularly. I found Annie to be a lovely person and very believable when she says, "Mother Mary says we must all learn to love our creator, God, and each other unconditionally." She states love is an essence and can cure all ills. "Love is more forceful than light and travels faster. There is no barrier." She further states that man doesn't know it yet but that love as an energy will replace gas and oil eventually. Divine love is an energy force and is as available as electricity — it's in the air. In fact, divine love, as energy, is the message of her book.

Just a few days ago I saw proof of it when I was shown a movie of Sai Baba in India. He says love is his message. I saw a film titled "The Miracle of Puttipar." It showed this enormous hospital, beautiful beyond description, built in one year. The architect was an Englishman and he described the plans taking five months and the hospital just seven months. Sai Baba had said it would have its first heart operation one year from the start, and it did indeed have its first operation one year from the dedication of the foundation of the building. It is an enormous, gorgeous place — miracle of all miracles. The hospital isn't even ten years old yet. Today it has six or seven heart operations every day. The infection rate is only 1% and the mortality rate 2%. People and doctors come from all over the world to see this fantastic miracle. The result of Sai Baba is love in action. Love is an energy that surpasses all else.

When movies of Sal Baba were brought to Yogacharya he would listen and watch with great interest and in later years many were brought to him from time to time. He would say nothing but he would always watch with great interest.

Sai Baba would send American devotees to Yogacharya and tell them that Yogacharya was their guru. There was a great similarity in their teachings — their great love and their great interest in teaching the young love and discipline.

If there is one sentence to sum up the life of Yogacharya and what he has meant to me, it is that he is and taught a love that is all encompassing, unconditional, and all empowering — it is love divine!

Afterword 1 – Irmgard Kurtz

(From a talk Irmgard Elizabeth Kurtz gave at Song of The Morning Ranch Sunday September 6, 1991 during Yogacharya's birthday remembrance.)

YOGACHARYA TOUCHED INNUMERABLE LIVES with his grace, his blessings, with his goodness, joy, and love. I am one of those blessed ones who had the great and good fortune to be able to be with Yogacharya for many years — both through his SRF work at the Detroit Institute of Arts and later here, (at Song of the Morning Ranch).

Today I would like to tell you — with Yogacharya's sweet permission — how I met him, this remarkable soul who became the greatest blessing, and also the greatest challenge of my life.

Thinking back, it seems as though we have always known each other, hut we actually met Thanksgiving weekend 1964. I had gotten started with the SRF lessons three and one-half years before, and had practiced the meditation techniques faithfully. However, there was one "small" problem: I had been rather seriously hurt during a bombing raid in Germany, years before. After a six-week hospital stay I thought all was well; but then over the next several years I started to develop headaches that became more excruciating as time went by, until our family physician scheduled me for "exploratory surgery" the week after Thanksgiving. I had written to the SRF Mother Center previously concerning this problem, and they advised me to go to Detroit SRF center to see Yogacharya J. Oliver Black.

Now, my then husband was so set against anything "yoga," that I could just as soon had planned a trip to the moon. In the meantime the surgery date moved closer, and I became quite concerned, thinking that there was not one "normal" brainwave to be found in me after practicing the Kriya Yoga techniques for about three years. So, at the suggestion from Mother Center on one hand, and urging from one of my Chicago SRF friends, my husband finally relented, just to get my mind off the surgery. And so I went.

I stayed overnight at my friend's place of the Chicago SRF group. We were leaving the following day for Detroit. Strangely, I was rather neutral about this upcoming visit. I knew nothing about Yogacharya, or Mr. Black, as we still called him then. So, not knowing what to expect, I took my famous "wait, look and listen" stance.

I slept in the meditation room on the couch that night, when early the following morning I awoke by something that felt as though I had been struck by lightning in the middle of my heart-center. I sat bolt-upright and looked to see what had happened. There, on the altar, the white robed picture of Yogacharya radiated light. And the picture and the radiating light kept expanding until it filled the whole room, and still the light expanded until there was no more meditation room left, no building, but throughout the sky all I could see was Yogacharya's face in this radiating light.

I don't know how long I sat there, watching, filled with joy and awe, and I couldn't wait after that to see this living master and saint.

Sunday morning found us at the Art Institute in Detroit. I was still totally shaken from this experience, and could hardly wait to see him face-to-face. Finally, a slender man, looking about 50, came out on the podium, wearing a dark blue suit, and sat down on the solitary chair. The place grew quiet. I wondered if this could be the same master I had seen in this ever-expanding light the morning before. I was now looking for a giant!! So I made the great mistake to search his face and looked intently at his spiritual eye. . . now, that was my first mistake, or my second blessing, because at the same time Yogacharya hooked his gaze, somehow, into my own spiritual eye and I "saw and felt" that he read and unrolled my whole life's history like a scroll. It seemed I viewed all the events of my life with him at the same time. That is quite an experience, and it can also be quite disconcerting. But at the same time I felt such love and compassion flowing from him to me, that it totally overwhelmed me, and I knew my search had ended, and I had found what I termed "the living light," and my spiritual home — and I knew I would never leave him again.

I don't remember much of the service — I was swimming in a sea of bliss and tears — and if that was not enough blessing, after the service, during our fellowship time, he also healed me of those excruciating headaches. Over my feeble protests that I was too heavy, he smiled and said he was a very strong yogi — he just lifted me up by the shoulders and neck, and cracked my head and neck a few times until I could feel the warmth of blood and life-force rushing through the left side of my head again. "Oh, it was just like a 'kink in a garden hose,'" yogi (Yogacharya) said afterwards,

When I tried to thank him, . . .And: "you'll be alright now!" — and I was! When I got home, still totally overwhelmed, all I had to do was to explain to my husband and my doctor why I no longer needed surgery, not exploratory, or otherwise. After some interesting discussions (!) They finally relented; I will count it to their honor: they agreed to re-do the tests — almost against their better judgment. Only this time the tests were all "normal."

And so, by the grace of god I was not only healed, but had found what I had been looking for all my life — a living master, and my spiritual home. This is my story, and it is true, every word of it. I have told this to some of my closest friends over the years, but mostly have kept this in my heart; now it can be told, that he who "walked with me and talked with me" was and is a very special, a very great soul. This is my tribute to you, sweet Yogacharyaji! Thank you for what you have taught me, thank you that you were here for all of us. Thank you master of mine, thank you for your light, your God-consciousness, your eternal love.

Irmgard (your devotee)

Afterword 2 – The Eternal in Us Cannot Die

By Peggy Braden

DEATH IS A TRANSITION, or so we're told. As I watched my yoga teacher draw his last breath, I doubted the helplessness of humanity in the face of death, and questioned even the finality of death itself.

A Biblical verse from the book of Job, which Handel set to music so beautifully in his oratorio Messiah, says: "O Death, where is Thy sting; O Grave, where is Thy victory?" It is set as a duet, as if two voices, representing humankind and death, are locked in an eternal struggle. In this scenario, the victory is won for humankind by the Son of God, a manifestation of the Eternal.

Another scripture, the Upanishads, holy to the Hindus, was often quoted by Yogacharya, (a name meaning "yoga teacher" and given to Oliver Black by Paramahansa Yogananda) especially in the months preceding his passing: "A mortal ripens like corn, and like corn he is born, again." It is a significant line in a story of a young man's efforts to outwit death and return to his family. He eventually succeeds in learning a carefully guarded secret from Yama, the god of Death himself, that the Eternal in man cannot die.

Yogacharya had talked for years about doing the "dipsy doodle" someday — meaning "leaving the body," or "dying." When he entered the hospital at age 96, he remarked to a long-time student, "This seems as good a place as any, doesn't it?" The student didn't quite know what Yogacharya meant at the time, but later reflected that he knew his time of departure was soon. Over the years he had quietly mentioned once in a while that he knew the year and day of his death.

On the second day of his hospital visit, September 16, 1989, I was happy to relieve his secretary at his bedside. I was to stay until the doctor arrived on rounds the next morning. Yogacharya was courteous and appreciative, as always. His many successful years at the helm of his own large auto parts business in Detroit and his great devotion to family and friends were products of his refined, gracious, yet down-to-earth nature. He had been a yoga teacher for over 50 years, founding a forested yoga retreat in northern Michigan in 1971. By 1989 he was the oldest living disciple of Yogananda.

Yogacharya ate and spoke little that day and spent much of his time sitting up with eyes closed and legs crossed in meditation posture. Later that evening I joined him in meditation, sitting on the bed across the room. The room was suffused with a stillness and deep spiritual peace. Although my own meditation was quite wonderful, I opened my eyes frequently to check on him, as the railings on the side of the bed were not up. He was strong, in good health, yet frail at 96. He had been sitting up and lying down under his own power all day. As the hour of mystic summoning approached, I glanced at him once more. Suddenly I saw him begin to fall backwards on the bed, eyes upturned and locked at the midspot between the eyebrows, his legs still folded in "sadhana" position. His breath was leaving him with the sound of a loud, hoarse whisper.

Feeling very calm, as if just a witness, I got up and went over to him. I very quietly called his name and ever so lightly touched his hand. I didn't want to shock him out of a deep state of meditation, if that was the case. But there is no immediate return for a yogi from the final state of meditation, or "mahasamadhi." It is their final exit from the body into the infinite Spirit. When there was no response from him I went for the nurse nearby. Not much later, the Herculean efforts of a team of doctors and nurses to revive him were of no avail. He had done the "dipsy doodle," just as he had joked about with his twinkling eyes and joyful laugh.

The transition now became ours as we adjusted to life without our dear friend and mentor. His yoga students from all over the country cooperated to keep his dream alive and thriving: his Song of the Morning yoga retreat. A play written to honor his last birthday, based on the teaching stories of Yogananda, contains a passage that was the theme of the play:

"Nay, but as one layeth his worn out robes away,
And taking new ones, sayeth, 'These will I wear today!'
So putteth by the spirit lightly its garb of flesh,
And passeth to inherit a residence afresh." – Bhagavad-Gita, Chapter 2

Yogacharya did not seem the victim of death, but rather met it on his terms — in meditation. His leaving seemed more a transition than a finality.

"Whenever a man gains greatness on this earth, he has his reward according to his meditation." – The Upanishads

About the Author

Evelyn "Betty" Howard was born of English parentage on January 12, 1924 in Halifax, Nova Scotia, Canada. She attended Halifax County Academy and took nurses' training at Victoria General Hospital in Halifax from 1942-1945. She then trained as a nurse anesthetist at Norwegian American Hospital in Chicago, Illinois. Betty worked as a registered nurse and nurse anesthetist in the Chicago area for 40 years.

Shortly after Betty finished her training she became interested in the yogic path. In 1959 she met the man who was to become her guru, Yogacharya J. Oliver Black. He was a direct disciple of Paramahansa Yogananda, who wrote the spiritual classic *Autobiography of a Yogi*. Betty has been influential in bringing many people to the teachings of yoga. She has earned the respect and gratitude of many she has helped. She led a weekly meditation class in her home in Chicago for twelve years which I had the opportunity to attend. For many years Betty helped aspiring yogis travel to the Detroit Institute of Arts to enjoy the Self-Realization Fellowship (SRF) Sunday services given by Yogacharya Oliver.

Betty now lives in Gaylord, Michigan, near Yogacharya's beloved Song of the Morning Ranch, "a Yoga Retreat of Excellence," where she regularly attends the meditations and Sunday services. The 800 acre retreat is nestled in the middle of the Pigeon River State Forest. It is a haven where spiritual aspirants can relax and meditate. Song of the Morning is now lovingly directed by Bob Raymer who was a great friend of

Yogacharya Oliver and a fellow disciple of Paramahansa Yogananda.

Angels Among Us has been written in memory of Yogacharya Oliver Black and is a testimony to Yogacharya's great influence on her life as well as many others who love him. This first printing is in honor of his 108 birthday commemoration celebration, September 1, 2001. Proceeds from the book will go into a fund for assisted living at Song of the Morning Ranch.

Lorne Dekun

Editor's note: Betty passed away in 2018; Bob Raymer passed away in 2008.

Blessings

from Yogacharya

In divine love,

Betty Howard

Made in the USA
Monee, IL
21 March 2022

93264342R00066